THE CATHOLIC UNIVERSITY OF AMERICA
CANON LAW STUDIES
Number 56

THE INTERDICT

A DISSERTATION

Submitted to the Faculty of Canon Law of the Catholic University of America in Partial Fulfillment of the Requirements for the Degree of

DOCTOR OF CANON LAW

BY

EDWARD JAMES CONRAN, A.B., J.C.L.
Priest of the Archdiocese of Philadelphia

THE CATHOLIC UNIVERSITY OF AMERICA
WASHINGTON, D. C.
1930

Nihil Obstat:

PHILIPPUS BERNARDINI, S.T.D., J.U.D.,
Censor Deputatus.
Washingtonii, D. C., die V Maii, 1930.

Imprimatur:

✠ D. CARD. DOUGHERTY,
Archiepiscopus Philadelphiensis.
Philadelphiae, die VIII Maii, 1930.

COMPOSED BY
MONOTYPE COMPOSITION CO., INC.
BALTIMORE, MD.

TABLE OF CONTENTS

FOREWORD

It is the purpose of this work to treat, as briefly as possible, of the nature, historical evolution and effects of the interdict. Consequently, this work does not pretend to be exhaustive.

The interdict, which may be inflicted either as a censure (medicinal penalty) or as a vindictive penalty, is one of the gravest and most severe canonical penalties inflicted by the Church. Although, unlike excommunication, the interdict does not separate the delinquent from the communion of the faithful, nevertheless, it deprives him of the use of certain sacred things, such as the Sacraments, the right to assist at divine services and ecclesiastical burial. It is evident, therefore, that the interdict is a very grave punishment.

In the early centuries of Christianity, the history of the interdict is difficult to trace, because in those times, the term *excommunication* was used to designate ecclesiastical punishments in general. In fact, at times, the various punishments are so closely connected, and the terminology is so unstable, that it is extremely difficult, if not impossible, to distinguish clearly between them. Consequently, during the early centuries, many punishments were called *excommunication,* which in reality were interdicts. An effort is made, therefore, to draw the line of demarcation between excommunication as such, and the interdict.

The dissertation is divided into two parts. The first part, which is divided into two chapters, has to do with the nature of the interdict and its historical evolution. The second part of the dissertation, which consists of eight chapters, treats of the effects of the interdict. In this commentary, each canon is treated according to the order in which it appears in the Code.

The writer takes advantage of the present occasion to express his sincere thanks to the members of the Faculty of Canon Law of the Catholic University for the kindly assistance rendered by them in the preparation of this work.

PART I

CHAPTER I

THE NATURE OF THE INTERDICT

According to its etymological signification, the term *interdict* denotes a prohibition of some kind. In Roman Law it was an interlocutory edict of the praetor usually in questions concerning property rights.[1] If the edict of the praetor directed an individual to do something, it was called a *decretum;* if such an edict commanded one to abstain from performing a certain act, it was an *interdictum.*[2] According to ecclesiastical law, it signifies the act of depriving, or the state of being deprived of the use of certain sacred things, and is defined as a censure by which the faithful, while remaining in communion with the Church, are forbidden the use of certain sacred things enumerated in subsequent canons.[3] Although the general term *censure* is here employed, the interdict may be inflicted as a vindictive penalty.[4] It is for this reason that D'Annibale[5] objects to the use of the term *censure* in defining the interdict; he, therefore, classifies it as a *prohibition,* whereby he intimates that it may be either a censure or a vindictive penalty.

An interdict is generally a species of censure, and a censure may be defined as a penalty by which a person baptized, delinquent and contumacious, is deprived of certain spiritual things until he ceases to be contumacious and is absolved.[6] Such a penalty, according to Canon 2215,

[1] Leage, *Roman Private Law,* p. 402 ff.
[2] Leage, *Roman Private Law,* p. 401.
[3] Can. 2268, n. 1.
[4] Can. 2291, nn. 1 and 2.
[5] *Summula Theologiae Moralis,* I, 369.
[6] Can. 2241, n. 1.

can be inflicted only by legitimate authority for the correction of the delinquent and as a punishment of the delict.

According to Canon 2286, vindictive penalties are those which are directly intended for the expiation of crimes, and, consequently, their relaxation does not depend on the mere cessation of contumacy. Such penalties are called *vindictive* because it is their primary purpose to avenge the public order.

A purely local interdict, or even a general personal interdict, inasmuch as the innocent are affected by them, would not be a censure, because a censure, properly so called, supposes a serious and morally imputable transgression. Consequently, Canon 2291 enumerates local interdicts and general personal interdicts among vindictive penalties. In like manner, the same Canon states that an interdict *ab ingressu ecclesiae*, may be inflicted as a vindictive penalty.

In very recent times, there was an interdict which was a vindictive penalty rather than a censure. Thus, the interdict inflicted by the Holy See upon the town of Adria in 1909 was a vindictive penalty, because it was inflicted for a period of fifteen days. Moreover, the interdict in question was both general local and general personal, which, according to Canon 2291, nn. 1 and 2, may be vindictive penalties. From the fact that the interdict ceased after the fifteen days had expired, it is evident that it was not a censure, because according to Canon 2248, §1, a censure once contracted, ceases only by absolution.[7]

Inasmuch as the interdict has been called a species of censure, it is evidently necessary to investigate into the character of censures in order to ascertain exactly what conditions are necessary to incur a censure, and, consequently, to incur the penalty of interdict.

The term *censure* in ecclesiastical nomenclature has a twofold signification; for it may be used in the sense signifying the prohibition against reading forbidden books; again, it is usually understood in the sense of a penalty imposed by ecclesiastical authority in punishment of a

---

[7] Cfr. *AAS*, I (1909), 765 ff.

delict.[8] In Roman law the term *censure* signified both the office and the sentence of a magistrate.[9] It was the duty of the magistrate to safeguard public morals, and consequently, to punish the offenders against public morality. Thus, the penalties inflicted by the magistrate were designated by the term *censure*.[10] It was but natural then that the ecclesiastical legislators should employ this same term to denote a like penalty. It is true, however, that besides the penal signification, the term *censure* also connoted the idea of a judgment or ordinance. Evidence of this is found in a letter of Pope Felix III (481–492) in which he writes: "...nec eorum expectanda poenitentia, quos excipit a coercitione *censura*." [11] The eighth Council of Toledo (653) speaks of a censure as the tie of an obligation. Thus the second canon of this Council states: "Tantum repetimus obligationis illic esse censuram." [12] The ninth Council of Toledo in 653, however, uses the term *censure* in the same sense in which it is employed today.[13] Although *censures* in ecclesiastical law generally meant a penalty such as excommunication, nevertheless, before the time of Pope Innocent III (1198–1216), the meaning and use of this term were not altogether stable. This is evident from a question to this great Pontiff as to the extent of the meaning of the term *censure:* "Quaerenti quid per censuram ecclesiasticam debeat intelligi, cum hujusmodi clausulam in nostris litteris apponimus; respondemus, quod per eam non solum interdicti, sed suspensionis, et excommunicationis sententia valeat intelligi..." [14] It is clear from this text that the term *censure,* from the time of Pope Innocent III, comprised the penalties of excommunication, suspension and interdict. This designation was accepted by Pope Gregory IX (1227–1241) in his Collection, and thereby

---

[8] Crnica, *Modificationes in Tract. de Censuris,* p. 2.

[9] Cod. Th. I, 1, 7.

[10] Crnica, *loc. cit.*

[11] Mansi, *Ampliss. coll. conc.* CV. 7, 1058.

[12] Mansi, 10, 1121.

[13] C. 10, Mansi, 11, 29.

[14] C. 20, X, *de significatione verborum,* V, 40.

obtained the force of law which it has continued to hold even to our own time.[15]

Thus, it is evident that in the present discipline of the Church, the term *censure* signifies the penalties of excommunication, suspension and interdict.

In the ancient laws of the Decretals no exact definition of a censure can be found, therefore canonists, in their efforts to define the expression, have recourse to various texts.[16] Thus, it happens that all authors do not define a censure in the same manner. Bonacina, for example, gives the following definition: "Censura est poena spiritualis, inflicta ab ecclesiastica potestate, privans hominem baptizatum usu aliquorum spiritualium per ordinem ad salutem." [17] The definition just given is not altogether accurate, because it mentions nothing about contumacy, and, therefore, does not differentiate between censures and vindictive penalties. Somewhat more accurate is the definition given by Lehmkuhl: "Censura est poena spiritualis et medicinalis, qua homo baptizatus delinquens et contumax per ecclesiasticam potestatem aliquorum bonorum spiritualium usu privatur." [18] This definition employing, as it does, the term *medicinalis,* clearly distinguishes between censures and vindictive penalties. The most adequate of all is the definition given by Reiffenstuel: "Censura, ut sic, est poena ecclesiastica spiritualis, medicinalis, per potestatem ecclesiasticam contumaciter delinquenti christiano inflicta, privans usu quorumdam bonorum spiritualium ad hoc, ut corrigatur, et a contumacia desistat."[19] The chief notion of the censure is that it is intended to be a medicinal penalty, and this idea is expressed in the last quoted definition in the phrase "ad hoc, ut corrigatur et a contumacia desistat."

Another important distinction between a censure and a vindictive penalty is that a censure, being medicinal, is inflicted for the purpose of destroying the contumacy of

---

[15] Crnica, *op. cit.*, p. 5.
[16] C. 11, X, *de constitution,* 1, 2; C. 1, *de sent. excom.* V, 11, in VI°.
[17] *De Censuris,* D. 1, q. 1, p. 1, n. 1.
[18] *Theologia Moralis,* t. 2, n. 861.
[19] *Jus Canonicum Universum,* lib. V, tit. XXXIX, n. 3.

the delinquent; and when this end is accomplished, the censure should necessarily cease; in other words, when the delinquent ceases to be contumacious and shows signs of sorrow he should be absolved by the Superior who imposed the censure.[20] A vindictive penalty, on the other hand, which is intended as a punishment for a delict, ceases either by the complete expiation of the delict, or by a dispensation granted by the Superior who imposed the penalty or by his competent Superior or successor.[21] Hence, it can be readily noticed that, when there is question of vindictive penalties, the removal of contumacy in the delinquent is not a sufficient cause for the removal of the penalty, which ceases when the time prescribed by the Superior has elapsed.[22]

But under the old legislation,[23] and the discipline of the Code,[24] censures, like other penalties, are either *latae sententiae* or *ferendae sententiae*, according as they are added to a law or precept in such a manner that they are *ipso facto* incurred upon the transgression of the law or precept in question, or are inflicted by a competent Superior or by an ecclesiastical judge.

Besides the division of censures just given, there is a further division into censures *a jure* and censures *ab homine.*[25] Thus, a censure is said to be *a jure* when a determinate punishment is established by the law itself for the violation thereof; this punishment may be either *latae* or *ferendae sententiae.* A censure is said to be *ab homine* when it is inflicted after the manner of a peculiar precept.

In the penal legislation of the Church, a distinction is also to be made between *reserved* censures and *non-reserved censures,* according as the power to absolve from them is, or is not withheld. Among such censures as are reserved, some are reserved to the Ordinary,[26] and others are reserved

---

[20] Can. 2236.
[21] Can. 2236.
[22] Crnica, *Modificationes in Tract.*, p. 6.
[23] C. 4, X, *de judiciis*, II, 1.
[24] Can. 2217, §1, n. 2.
[25] Can. 2217, §1, n. 3.
[26] Can. 2256, §2.

to the Holy See.[27] Furthermore, among the censures reserved to the Holy See, some are reserved *simpliciter;* others, *speciali modo,* from which priests cannot absolve, unless they obtain special faculties to do so from the Holy See. According to the legislation of the Code, certain censures are reserved *specialissimo modo* to the Holy See.[28]

To incur a censure, one must be baptized, delinquent and contumacious. Hence, first of all, the delinquent must be a baptized person, because by Baptism alone can a person become subject to the laws of the church, and, consequently, liable to the punishments which the violation of those laws entails.[29] Moreover, to incur a censure, one, besides being baptized, must be delinquent; in other words, he must be guilty of an external and morally imputable transgression of a law or precept, to which is added at least an indeterminate canonical sanction.[30] Finally, to incur a censure, the delinquent must be contumacious, for it is the very purpose of the censure to correct the stubborn transgressor of the law.

The sacred things of which the interdicted person or persons may be deprived are: (a) the liturgical services, (b) certain sacraments and sacramentals,[31] and (c) Christian burial.[32]

The prohibition from the use of the sacred things mentioned, admits of degrees according as the cases differ.[33] The interdict does not deprive one of all the privileges of membership in the Church. Unlike excommunication, it does not separate one from the communion of the faithful, nor does it necessarily take away jurisdiction.[34] Therefore, the essential difference between excommunication and the interdict, lies in the fact that an interdict does not separate the delinquent from the communion of the Church.[35] Again,

[27] *Ibidem.*
[28] Can. 2245, §3.
[29] Canons, 12, 87.
[30] Can. 2195.
[31] Can. 2275, n. 2; Can. 2265.
[32] Ojetti, *Synopsis*, II, col. 2368.
[33] Aryinhac, *Penal Legislation of the New Code*, p. 128.
[34] Ojetti, *loc. cit.*
[35] Genicot, *Theologia Moralis*, II, n. 622.

an interdict does not necessarily presuppose a personal fault, because it may fall upon a moral, as well as upon a physical body, or upon a place. In all these respects, it differs from excommunication; nevertheless, in effect, they are sometimes much the same.

The interdict is also quite different from the censure of suspension. The latter deprives clerics of the use of ecclesiastical powers peculiar to them, while the interdict deprives one of the spiritual goods common to all the faithful.[36]

A special warning is given in Canon 2214, §2, to all those having the power to inflict censures, that they should make a sober and prudent use of this power, especially when there is question of such censures as are incurred automatically *(latae sententiae)*. Perhaps it will not be amiss to re-state the warning of the Council of Trent in this connection:

> Meminerint Episcopi aliique Ordinarii se pastores non percussores esse, atque ita praeesse sibi subditis oportere, ut non in eis dominentur, sed illos tanquam filios et fratres diligant elaborentque ut hortando et monendo ab illicitis deterreant, ne ubi deliquerint, debitis eos poenis coercere cogantur; quos tamen si quid per humanam fragilitatem peccare contigerit, illa Apostoli est ab eis servanda praeceptio ut illos arguant, obsecrent, increpent in omni bonitate et patientia cum saepe plus erga corrigendos agat benevolentia quam austeritas, plus exhortatio quam comminatio, plus caritas quam potestas; sin autem ob delicti gravitatem virga opus erit, tunc cum mansuetudine rigor, cum misericordia iudicium, cum lenitate severitas adhibenda est, ut sine asperitate disciplina, populis salutaris ac necessaria, conservetur et qui correcti fuerint, emendentur aut, si resipiscere noluerint, ceteri, salubri in eos animadversionis exemplo, a vitiis deterreantur." [37]

---

[36] Aryinhac, *loc. cit.*

[37] Trid., *sess.* XIII, *de ref.*, cap. I.

An interdict is *local* when it directly affects a place in which the use of sacred things is forbidden;[38] hence, a local interdict only indirectly affects the persons living in the interdicted place; for if they leave the territory which is under a local interdict, they are not affected by it, unless, of course, they themselves be also under a *personal* interdict. A *personal* interdict is that which directly affects the person, and follows him wheresoever he goes. It may also happen that an interdict be local and at the same time personal; such an interdict is called *mixed* or *deambulatory*.[39] Interdicts of this type were frequently used in various places in which bishops, unjustly deprived of their liberty, were held captive.[40]

Both personal and local interdicts may be particular or general. The *particular personal interdict* is imposed upon a certain determinate person or upon several persons expressly mentioned.[41] The *general personal interdict* is that which is imposed on a body of individuals, for instance, on the clergy of a diocese. Such an interdict affects the body as such, and the individual members inasmuch as they form part of the body.

A *particular local interdict* is laid on some individual sacred place, as for example, on a parish church or on a cemetery. If all the churches in a given city were interdicted individually, the interdict in each case would be a *particular local interdict*.[42] A *general local interdict* is that which affects an entire diocese, province, state or nation.[43] This last named interdict, therefore, affects every church and sacred place in the interdicted territory.[44]

Finally, attention must be given to the interdict from entering a church *(interdictum ab ingressu ecclesiae)*, which one must be careful not to confound with *suspension from entering a church (suspensio ab ingressu*

---

[38] Alterii, *De Censuris*, II, p. 287.

[39] Devoti, lib. IV, *Institutionum Can.*, tit. XIX, n. 2.

[40] Council of Cologne (1266), Can. IV, Mansi, 23, 1136.

[41] Devoti, *loc. cit.*

[42] Suarez, *De Censuris*, lib. XXXII, n. 10.

[43] Devoti, *loc. cit.*

[44] Lega, *Praelectiones De Judiciis Eccl.*, pars. I, tit. V, n. 319.

ecclesiae). By the former is meant a prohibition against entering a church for the purpose of celebrating or assisting at Mass or any other divine service.[45] It might be well to explain exactly what is meant by the term *church* as here employed. A church is any temple or sacred place set apart by the bishop for public worship.[46] Hence, a person interdicted from entering a church, may enter a private oratory, semi-public or public oratory,[47] and there celebrate Mass or other divine functions, or assist at them. Moreover, a person thus interdicted may even enter a church, as defined above, in order to pray there, provided, of course, that Mass or any other divine function is not actually being celebrated there. The suspension from entering a church, on the other hand, is the same as suspension *a divinis*, which, in the old law, was a suspension from the acts of *orders* and not of *jurisdiction*.[48] The term *Suspensio ab ingressu ecclesiae*, is abrogated by the Code.

[45] Smith, *Elements of Eccl. Law*, III, n. 3338; Vermeersch-Creusen, *Epitome*, III, n. 478.

[46] Can. 1161.

[47] Can. 1188.

[48] Smith, *Ibidem*.

CHAPTER II

Historical Development of the Interdict

The word *interdict* connotes the idea of a negative command. "In general it means the act of a person forbidding something. As here understood, the interdict means a regular correctional punishment of the Church, by which, in punishment of a crime, the public celebration of divine service (officia divina), the administration of certain sacraments, and ecclesiastical burial are forbidden in certain places or to certain individuals." [1]

It is a fact to be admitted by all that any society, if it is to perdure, must exercise the right of punishing refractory and recalcitrant members. This punishment is carried on by denying to such members some or all of the privileges, or even by depriving them of membership itself. Thus, it is clear that every society, large or small, does exercise and must exercise this right, not only to protect the reputation of the society but even to insure its very existence.

Now the Church, although the highest type of society, is no exception to this general rule. The Church, although divinely founded, is an external organization of individual members, and for that reason, often finds herself confronted with the same problems as confront the state and other human societies. Thus, from the very beginning of Christianity, the Church has been forced to impose such severe punishments as excommunication, and even general excommunication, the latter of which may be considered as a severe form of interdict. In fact, it will be seen later, that the severe punishments of general excommunication gradually moderated into the general local interdict.

[1] Smith, *op. cit.*, n. 3329.

Section I.—Pre-Christian Interdicts

It was a common belief among the early pagans that persons placed under ban for any offense against the gods or the state, were to be shunned by all. Furthermore, those who, in any way, associated with those under ban, might arouse the anger of the gods, and consequently, be visited with the most dire punishments.[2] Thus, among the early Greeks, those guilty of bloodshed, were deprived of purification with holy water.[3] This punishment is quite similar to our Christian interdict, inasmuch as it deprives the delinquent of some spiritual goods. The Roman State interdicted the traitor from fire and water.[4] In like manner, the Druids excluded the disobedient from participation in any religious ceremony.[5] Nor was this idea foreign to the Hebrews; for after Esdras had called an assembly of the Jews after the return from the captivity, it was decreed that he who refused to come, "all his substance should be taken away." [6] In effect, this privation from all his substance was an interdict, because, like the Christian interdicts, it deprived the offender of the use of certain goods. It now remains to be seen that the Christian Church, especially in her infancy, had to adopt similar measures for the purpose of protecting her external organization.

Section II.—The Interdict in the Christian Church

That the Catholic Church, from the earliest times, possessed the right of punishing stubborn offenders against decency and morality, is a fact confirmed by history itself. These punishments were more or less severe, according to the gravity of the crime itself, or to the obstinacy of the delinquent. Thus, even in Apostolic times, excommunication, the most severe of all church punishments, was not unknown; for the Sacred Scriptures relate that Saint Paul

[2] *Encyc. Brit.*, Vol. X, art., "Excommunication."
[3] Demosthenes, *Orations*, 505, 14 (ΠΡΟΣ ΛΕΠΤΙΝΑΝ).
[4] Krehbiel, *The Interdict*, p. 4.
[5] Caesar, *De Bello Gallico*, VI, 13.
[6] I Esdras, X, 8.

excommunicated the incestuous man of Corinth.[7] There is indeed a likelihood that the various punishments of the early Christian Church were not unlike those of Hebrew worship. Nevertheless, it must be remembered that the right of the Church to castigate her disobedient children, is inherent in her very nature, inasmuch as she was established by Jesus Christ as a perfect society for the salvation of souls.[8] Therefore, it is clear that the Church did not derive her penal system from the Hebrews, but, on the contrary, it is patent that the power to punish delinquents is a necessary means to that end for which the Church was established, i.e., the salvation of souls.[9] Moreover, if, as all admit, the power to punish its offending members, belongs to any secular society, whose aim at best is the attainment of some temporal good, it certainly follows that the Church, whose sole aim is the eternal salvation of mankind, certainly must possess and must use this right with a view of reclaiming the wayward sheep back into the fold.

Since the work of saving souls must continue until the end of time, Christ established His Church as a perfect society, so that the work begun by Him might be perpetuated. Thus, He promised and gave to the Church all the power necessary for the attainment of this end. For, He conferred on Saint Peter the supreme power of ruling and governing the faithful.[10] Moreover, Christ charged the same Apostle with the care of feeding all His sheep.[11] The other Apostles were commissioned with the duty of preaching the Gospel to every creature, baptizing them and teaching them to observe all things, whatsoever He had commanded them.[12] In like manner, He gave to His Apostles the power of loosing and binding, with the promise that whatsoever they should loose or bind on earth, He would loose or bind in heaven.[13] In other words, the sen-

[7] I Cor. I, 5.

[8] Solieri, *Institutiones Juris Ecclesiastici,* p. 36.

[9] Cavagnis, *Institu. Juris. Pub. Eccles.,* I, n. 46.

[10] *Matth.,* XVI, 18 ff.

[11] *John,* XXI, 15 ff.

[12] *Matth.,* XXVIII, 19 ff.

[13] *Matth.,* XVIII, 18.

tence of the Apostles was to receive the same ratification in heaven, as if Christ Himself had pronounced it. The reason for this is clear, because the power whereby the Apostles ruled the Church was received from Christ Himself, and when the Apostles act, Christ acts; when they speak, Christ speaks. For He said to them: "He that heareth you, heareth Me; and he that despiseth you despiseth Me." [14] Likewise, in speaking of fraternal correction, Christ said: "And if he will not hear the Church, let him be to thee as a heathen and publican." [15]

From what has been said, it is certainly patent that supreme power was given by Christ to His Church, and without doubt, this supreme power embraces the right to impose censures on offending members of the Church. That the Apostles themselves fully recognized that they possessed the right and power to impose censures, is evident from Saint Paul's Epistle to the Corinthians: "For the weapons of our warfare are not carnal; but mighty until the pulling down of fortifications, destroying counsels. . . and having in readiness to revenge all disobedience, when your obedience shall be fulfilled." [16] Moreover, Saint Paul made use of this power: ". . . Of whom is Hymeneus and Alexander, whom I have delivered up to Satan, that they may learn not to blaspheme." [17] Likewise, in his Epistle to the Galatians, Saint Paul writes: "And as we said before, so now I say again: 'If anyone preach to you a gospel, besides that which you have received, let him be anathema.' " [18] From these texts it is clear that the great Apostle not only recognized his power to impose censures, but that he actually exercised this power.

Moreover, the opinion denying the right of the Church to inflict penalties, has been frequently condemned. Thus, Pope Martin V in the year 1418, condemned the various errors of Wicleff.[19] In like manner, Pope Leo X in the

---

[14] *Luke,* X, 16.
[15] *Matth.,* XVIII, 17.
[16] II Cor. X, 4 ff.
[17] I Tim., I, 20.
[18] I, 9.
[19] Denzinger-Bannwart, n. 491 ff.

year 1520, condemned the heretical teaching of Luther on this point.[20]

It must be carefully borne in mind, however, that, although Christ gave the Church the power to inflict censures, He, nevertheless, did not institute each single species of censure; but the fact remains that Christ gave full power to the Church, and ordained that the Church should employ this power in such a manner as would be most conducive to the end for which the Church was established.

To support the above contention it is sufficient to read the Gospel narrative to ascertain that Christ gave this power to Saint Peter and the other Apostles, and through them to their successors, when He said: "Whatsoever you shall bind on earth, shall be bound also in heaven; and whatsoever you should loose upon earth, shall be loosed also in heaven." [21] By this text is understood primarily that Christ gave to His Apostles the power to remit sins; nevertheless, the meaning of this text must not be limited to the power of forgiving sins, for the words of Christ are universal in their content. Therefore it is evident that Christ conferred not only the power of forgiving sins, but also the power to use the means necessary for the attainment of that end. For it is a known fact that only by penalties and hardships, are certain offenders brought to a sense of duty, and to a realization of the enormity of their offenses. Furthermore, there is no reason why a limit should be placed on the meaning of the words which Christ Himself in no way limited. Therefore, it is clear that the power granted by Christ to the pastors of the Church, was so extended as to include even the power to exclude from its membership recalcitrant subjects.[22]

Section III.—The Exercise of the Penal Power in the Early Church

After it is ascertained that the Church, from the beginning, possessed the power of punishing obstinate offenders,

[20] Denzinger-Bannwart, n. 763 ff.
[21] *Matth.*, XVIII, 18.
[22] Hyland, *Excommunication*, p. 14 ff.

the question as to when this power was first exercised will naturally arise. The origin of the interdict has been the subject of much controversy among canonists who, for the most part, have centered their attention on the subject with a view of arriving at a knowledge of the legal and juridical character of the interdict, rather than from a point of view of historical development.[23] Thus, some authors contend that interdicts were in full force in the early days of the Church,[24] while others deny their common use before the tenth century. The fact remains, however, that both arguments have an element of truth; but to assert that the canonical interdict, as understood today, originated in either the first century or the tenth century, is an assertion which, to say the least, is difficult to prove. In order to arrive at some satisfactory conclusion, it must be kept in mind that the interdict had a very gradual development, and for this reason, it is extremely difficult, if not impossible, to state exactly in which century the interdict came into use.

Another important fact to be remembered, is that in the early centuries of Christianity the term *excommunication* was employed to designate ecclesiastical punishments in general. It is, therefore, very easy to understand how a controversy could arise regarding the origin of the interdict. Many punishments in the early Church were quite similar to the interdict, and yet were classified as excommunication. In this connection, Cappello [25] makes a distinction worthy of note; he argues that there were indications of personal interdicts from the early days of Christianity, while the local interdict came into use during the tenth century. Thus, in the fifth and sixth centuries, persons guilty of public crimes, such as impurity or perjury, were forbidden to receive the Holy Eucharist, or to enter a church for the purpose of assisting at divine services. This punishment lasted either for a fixed time, v.g., one year, or for an indefinite period; in other words, until such time as the offenders showed signs of emendation.[26] Smith calls this

[23] Howland, *Interdict*, A. H. A. Report, 1899.I, 433.
[24] Smith, *op. cit.*, n. 3330.
[25] *De Censuris*, p. 142.
[26] C. 24, D. CXI, q. 3.

punishment a partial interdict.[27] He further states that only in the eleventh century did the canonical interdict receive its full canonical development.[28]

If, as has been stated, the Church punished unruly members with excommunication even from the earliest days of Christianity, when the Christian membership was small, the use of this means of punishment naturally and necessarily increased with the constantly growing number of Christians.[29]

Section IV.—Evolution of General Punishments.

After the Church had triumphantly emerged from the great persecutions, it was but natural that she should exercise her authority more fully in the external management of her Mission. The imperial recognition of Christianity gave the Church a reputation which she had to take great care to sustain. It is therefore a fact worthy of note that the same century which marked the legalizing of the Christian belief, was the same century in which the first recorded case of general excommunication occurred.[30] Hence, for the first time, a group of persons were excluded from membership in the Church by a single censure. It happened that Saint Basil threatened an entire village with excommunication because a girl had been kept there by force against the will of her guardians.[31] In this case it seems that the ravisher must have been abetted and protected by the people of the village; consequently the whole village was forced to share the punishment. The introduction of this new form of censure gives an indication that the time had now come when excommunication of individuals no longer suited the needs of the time, and the adoption of a more effective discipline was now in order. The case just related, may be quoted by some as a proof that the general local interdict had its origin in the fourth century. This

[27] *Op. cit.*, n. 3330.

[28] *Ibidem.*

[29] Krehbiel, *The Interdict*, p. 4.

[30] Krehbiel, *op. cit.*, p. 5.

[31] Howland, *op. cit.*, I, 433.

opinion, however, is sharply contested by Kober [32] who contends that the letter of Saint Basil does not contain any real sentence or threat of interdict as the term is understood today. He likewise states that the letter of Saint Basil merely relates that a priest in a rural parish was severely reprehended for not taking more earnest and energetic action with a view of bringing the kidnappers to justice. It seems that crimes of this kind were quite common at that time, which fact explains the reason for the reprimand. In his letter, Saint Basil commands the priest to do all in his power to restore the girl to her parents, and to punish the kidnappers with excommunication from public prayers for a period of three years; moreover, similar punishment was to be inflicted on the accomplices of the kidnappers and upon their families. This letter of Saint Basil even contained a threat of excommunication against the entire village, when it had retained the girl, and by force resisted attempts towards her deliverance.[33] Kober argues that this form of punishment was employed before, and that it cannot be classified as a canonical interdict. His contention is based on the fact that Saint Basil merely commanded the priest, who neglected his duty, to excommunicate the actual kidnapper, a punishment which was explicitly contained in the words of the text. The accomplices were to be excluded from public prayers for a space of three years. Hence, it is evident that it was the intention of Saint Basil to inflict a milder form of punishment upon the accomplices. It was further provided that the families of the accomplices were to share this excommunication from public prayers, only if they were connected with the crime. Kober [34] maintains that no one suffered any punishment save through his own misdeed. Moreover, he contends that the very fact that only those who aided or abetted the actual culprit and his accomplices were excluded from public prayers and placed among the *flentes*, is proof that public worship itself did not cease, but continued as it did prior

---

32 "Das Interdikt," *AkKR*, XXI, 4.

33 *Epist.* CCLXX,—*MPG*, 32, 1002-1003.

34 *Op. cit.*, p. 5.

to the affair, otherwise, there would be no need of depriving the guilty parties from public prayers.

It seems to be on this point that a misunderstanding as to the meaning of the words of Saint Basil has arisen. It must be remembered that he ordered the entire village to be excommunicated only if it received the kidnapped person, held her a captive, or refused to deliver her to her parents. There is question here of an entirely different kind of participants in the crime. The people of the village, while they had no actual part in the crime, nevertheless, because they held the kidnapped person a prisoner, are to be excommunicated from public prayers exactly as the actual accomplices, because of their forcible resistance. Moreover, they should be made to realize the enormity of the crime, so that in the future, instead of assisting even passively in a crime of this kind, they would endeavor to prevent it.

Even in this rather extraordinary instance, although punishment was threatened to the entire village, nevertheless, it is clear that it was not the intention of Saint Basil to suspend worship in the churches, thereby depriving all in general of the comforts and solace of Religion. It is in this point that the general punishment of the entire village differs essentially from a general local interdict. That public services were not suspended, is evident from the very fact that the actual kidnapper and his accomplices were excluded from all public prayers; otherwise, what need would there be of depriving certain individuals of something of which they, as members of the entire body, had already been deprived? It seems inaccurate, therefore, to consider this punishment as an interdict.

In the opinion of Crnica,[35] the first example or trace of a general local interdict is found in the latter part of the sixth century. In the year 566, a villa belonging to the church of Saint Metrias was usurped by King Childeric. The bishop of the city, unable to compel the offender to repair the damage done, approached the church of Saint Metrias and praying before the tomb of the Saint, said: "No light

[35] *Modificationes in Tract. de Censuris*, p. 136.

shall burn here, nor shall Psalms be chanted, most glorious Saint, until you avenge the evil deeds of your enemies, and restore the property taken by violence, to the Holy Church."[36] After he had done this, he threw branches containing sharp thorns over the tomb, and ordered the doors of the church closed. This act on the part of the bishop certainly has every likeness of an interdict, because he ordered the doors of the church to be closed, and consequently, entrance therein was forbidden to all. Moreover, divine services were not to be celebrated in the church until such time as full restitution had been made. It might be argued that this example does not contain all the circumstances and consequences of the interdict which were inflicted in later centuries; nevertheless, that this example contains the essential elements of an interdict cannot be denied.[37]

Another excellent example, which was perhaps the first real case of a general local interdict, is to be found in Rouen, France, in the year 586. On Easter Sunday of that year, Praetextatus, Archbishop of the city, was assassinated while performing the solemn services in connection with the great feast. Whereupon, Leudovaldus, the Bishop of Bayeux, who had taken charge of the diocese, ordered all the churches of the city to be closed, *"ut in his populus solemnia divina non spectaret, donec indagatione communi reperiretur hujus actor sceleris."*[38] Kober[39] calls this the first real example of an interdict. It must be remembered, however, that the fact that the people were deprived of divine services, since the doors of the church were closed against them, does not prove that divine services were not privately celebrated at least for clerics.[40] When one considers the condition and circumstances of the times, however, he cannot help but admit that it was scarcely possible that divine services were held at all, if the general faithful were excluded, because the private celebration of divine

[36] Gregory of Tours, *De gloria confess.*, *MPL*, 71, 879.
[37] Kober, *op. cit.*, p. 11.
[38] Gregory of Tours, *Historia Francor.*, I, 8, *MPL*, 71, 471.
[39] *AkKR*, XXI, 8.
[40] Crnica, *op. cit.*, p. 137.

services was really something entirely unknown in those times.[41] Hence, it seems safe to conclude that the celebration of divine services was forbidden when the faithful were excluded from them. Kober[42] holds that this action was the imposition of a real local interdict in the strict sense of the term, because of the fact that divine services were suspended, and because the entire city was punished because of a crime supposedly committed at the instigation of the queen. Crnica[43] considers the punishment in question as a real interdict, because, he argues, that the exclusion of the faithful from divine services is the principal effect of a general local interdict. This opinion, however, is not held by all; for Van Espen[44] argues that Leudovaldus, acting as the administrator of the Archdiocese, ordered the churches closed because of the fact that the faithful of Rouen held ill feelings against the murdered Archbishop, on account of his relentless warfare against crime; it is further urged by Van Espen that the queen was suspected of having instigated the crime. It seems that he holds the opinion that the faithful were punished only because of the fact that they disliked the Archbishop, and because this dislike had an indirect effect, at least, in his assassination. Kober[45] is loath to accept an interpretation of this kind; for he argues that the very manner in which Saint Gregory narrates the event, allows little room for the assumption of Van Espen. Evidence was certainly not wanting to show that the queen was enraged against the Archbishop, and it was by reason of her unrelenting hatred against him that she was suspected of having instigated the crime. Moreover, it is related that the inhabitants in general mourned for him in the most sincere fashion, and that one of the older inhabitants openly charged the queen with being the original framer of the crime: "... Unus senior ad Fredegundem veniens ait: Multa enim mala in hoc saeculo perpetrasti, sed adhuc pejus non feceras, quam ut sacerdotem Dei

---

[41] Crnica, *Ibidem.*
[42] *Op. cit.*, XXI, 8.
[43] *Op. cit.*, p. 137.
[44] *Tractatus de Censuris Eccl.*, c. IX, §3.
[45] *Loc. cit.*

juberes interfici. Sit Deus ultor sanguinis innocentis velociter; nam et omnes erimus inquisitores mali hujus, ut tibi diutius non liceat tam crudelia exercere." [46] Hence, Kober [47] asks how can anyone, after considering the facts of the case, maintain that this interdict was inflicted on the people and not on the queen?

Almost coincident with the murder of Pratetextatus, trouble arose in a convent at Poitiers as a result of the removal of the prioress. It happened that Chrodieldis, one of the nuns, caused the prioress to be removed, because Chrodieldis, herself, wished to become prioress. The entire affair was carried on in a most unlawful and disgraceful manner. In order to realize her ambition of becoming prioress, the nun left the cloister with forty others, and with the aid of a group of lawless laymen had the convent besieged and plundered, and the prioress was taken and held captive. These events occurred a few days before Easter Sunday; therefore the bishop seized the occasion to notify Chrodieldis that the prioress must be released at once, otherwise he would not celebrate the Easter ceremonies at Poitiers, nor would any catechumen be permitted to receive Baptism. Saint Gregory of Tours gives the following account: *"Haec autem gesta sunt ante septem dies Paschae. Cumque episcopus haec omnia graviter ferret nec valeat seditionem diabolicam mitigare, misit ad Chrodieldem dicens: relinque abbatissam, ut in his diebus in hoc carcere non retineatur; alioquin non celebrabo Pascha Domini, neque baptismum in hac urbe unus catechumenus obtinebit, nisi abatissa a vinculo, quo tenetur, iubeatur absolvi."* [48] In this instance there is certainly a threat of interdict of the most severe type; since it was in force during the Easter season. It is also clear that there was a threat of interdict, since the bishop warned the offender that divine services would cease unless the prioress was restored to liberty.[49]

---

[46] Gregory of Tours, *Historia Francor., loc. cit.*

[47] *AkKR*, XXI, 9.

[48] *Histor. Francor.*, I, 10, c. 15—*MPL*, 77, 545.

[49] Crnica, *op. cit.*, p. 138.

Another interesting example of an interdict is to be found in a dispute over a plot of ground belonging to the Church of Agde. It seems that the ground in question was unjustly taken over for the use of a certain individual, and Leo, Bishop of the city, demanded its return. At first the offender was loath to comply with the demand of the bishop, but later, having been stricken with serious illness, he consented to make restitution. Although he regained his health, he did not fulfill his promise, but instead, went so far as to make threats against the bishop. As he had no other way of enforcing his mandate, Leo went in person to the church, cast himself in front of the relics of the Apostle Andrew, and spent the entire night in deep sorrow.[50] On the following day, he drew near the lamps which were suspended over the arches, and smashing them with a staff, declared that no light should burn there until God had avenged the crime, and had the property of the church restored. An important fact is to be noted here: if no divine services were celebrated in those times without the burning of lights, it is clear, since the lamps were broken, that divine services were impossible under the circumstances. Therefore the action on the part of the bishop can be interpreted only as declaring a general interdict. Moreover, it is observed by Kober,[51] the manner in which these interdicts were imposed shows that they were of rather frequent occurrence, nor does there seem to be the slightest indication that these punishments were looked upon as innovations.

An extraordinary example of the interdict was that imposed by Bishop Hincmar of Laon. This bishop, on account of his misconduct, was ordered to appear before a synod held in the year 869. Fearing lest he should be condemned, he ordered the priests of his diocese to abstain from celebrating Mass, from administering the Holy Eucharist; he even went so far as to forbid Baptism to infants even though they be in danger of death; moreover he prohibited the burying of the dead. Thus, Hincmar, Archbishop of

[50] Kober, *AkKR,* XXI, 10.

[51] *Op. cit.,* XXI, 11.

Rheims, in a letter to the younger Hincmar, writes: "...praecipisti, ut in commissa tibi paroechia nemo Missam cantaret, nemo communionem sacram perciperet..., praecipisti quoque, ut nemo parvulos etiam mortis urgente periculo in tua parochia baptizaret..., vetuisti, ut nemo quemquam ad ultimam poenitentiam vel reconciliationem reciperet vel poscenti ultimo sacrae communionis viatico subveniret..., jussisti maximam inhumanitatem, ut nemo mortuum in tua paroechia sepeliret." [52] As the younger Hincmar had feared, he was cast into prison.[53] According to his uncle, the Metropolitan of Rheims, the interdict was actually carried out.[54] It was provided in the interdict that no divine services should be celebrated in the diocese of Laon while the bishop should be in prison.

Being greatly perturbed by this unreasonable and rash procedure on the part of his nephew, the Archbishop of Rheims sent admonitions to him in prison and declared that by his metropolitan power he would prevent the interdict from being further carried out. It must be borne in mind that this severe condemnation was not upon the interdict itself, but upon the abuse made of it. "Ideo et vituperatur Hincmarus Laudunensis a Hincmaro Remensi Archiepiscopo et cognato suo, propter istum hucusque inauditum inhumanitatis actum, praesertim quia hoc fecerat propter injurias proprias, imo etiam prius quam eaedem ipsi irrogarentur." [55] It can scarcely be imagined that a man of the learning of Hincmar of Rheims did not know that the interdict, with all its effects, had long been in use, and unless it was abused it was never condemned or even questioned by anyone.[56] From this fact it is clear that the interdict was a recognized mode of punishment at that time.

A chronicler named Ademar narrates that in the year 994, Bishop Alduin of Limoges pronounced an interdict on his diocese because of many robberies committed by various

[52] Hardouin, V, 1373, Epist. III, ad Hincmar Lauden.

[53] Kober, *op. cit.*, XXI, 13.

[54] Kober, *Ibidem.*

[55] Crnica, *op. cit.*, p. 139.

[56] Kober, *op. cit.*, XXI, 16.

knights.[57] Thus, all services were forbidden in churches and cloisters, so that the faithful were altogether deprived of the solace of religion. It was the banditry of these knights which prompted the famous resolutions of the Synod of Limoges which convened in the year 1031.[58] In this Council it was decreed that if the robbers did not reform, the entire territory would be punished with general excommunication in such a manner that no one save clerics, strangers and children under two years of age shall receive burial; moreover the services in the churches were to be conducted in a low tone of voice. It was further decreed that Penance and Viaticum could be administered only at the hour of death.[59] In this instance there is a clear example of a general local interdict extending over an entire district and brought about by the misdeeds of certain lawless knights.

From all the foregoing examples it is evident that prior to the tenth and eleventh centuries there were punishments which contained the essential character of the local interdict. It is true that the earlier examples do not possess the same evident indications of an interdict, but in the course of time there was a gradual evolution until the eleventh century, when the interdict reached the stage of full development. It seems to be for this reason that the interdict is sometimes thought to have its origin in the eleventh century. One great change in the history of the interdict becomes very apparent at this time, and this change is due to the fact that interdicts are applied with much greater frequency, and upon entire districts, provinces and nations.[60] Likewise, in the beginning, the interdict appeared without any special name. Furthermore, even as late as the eleventh century, this punishment was known by the name of "excommunication of churches," although as a punishment it was fully developed.[61] In the earlier cen-

[57] Bouquet, *Recueil des Historiens des Gaules et de la France*, t. 10, p. 147.

[58] Kober, *op. cit.*, XXI, 16.

[59] Hardouin, VI, 885.

[60] Kober, *op. cit.*, XXI, 17.

[61] Crnica, *op. cit.*, p. 140.

turies, either the effects of an interdict were not determined, or absolutely every sacred function was forbidden; but after the eleventh century, the sentence of interdict nearly always indicated what was forbidden during the interdict and what was permitted. Thus, in the Council of Limoges in the year 1031, Abbot Odolric urged that an interdict be imposed because certain princes who violated the "Truce of God."[62] The effects of the proposed interdict were enumerated with great detail. Thus, the sentence of interdict as proposed by Abbot Odolric provided that unless the knights would acquiesce to peace, the entire territory of Limoges would be placed under *public excommunication,* in such a way that no one, excepting clerics and infants under two years of age, could receive burial; it was further provided that the altars in the churches must be stripped of crucifixes and ornaments in order to indicate mourning as on Good Friday; the altars were to be recovered only while Mass was being celebrated behind closed doors; during the period of *excommunication,* no one could enter the state of Matrimony, nor could the "Kiss of Peace" be given; finally, only such food could be taken as was permitted during the season of Lent.[63] In this example it is clear that the punishment in question was a general local interdict, although it is expressly called *excommunication.*

Many examples of the interdict may be found in the eleventh century and thereafter, because of their continued frequency. Thus, Pope Gregory VII gave authority to the bishops of France to suspend all celebration of divine services on account of the numerous crimes committed by King Philip I of that country.[64] In like manner, Pope Gregory, himself, pronounced a sentence of interdict upon the province of Posen, because King Boleslaus had murdered Bishop Stanislaus while he was celebrating divine services.[65]

It is certain that in the eleventh century there was a clear distinction between the penalty of excommunication and

---

[62] Mansi, 19, 541.

[63] Hardouin, VI, 885.

[64] Hardouin, VI, 1264, *Epist.* 1, 2, 5.

[65] Crnica, *op. cit.*, p. 140.

that of interdict, although the latter was even in this comparatively late period, sometimes called *excommunication.* Thus, the Council of Poitiers in 1078, makes the following statement: "Si vero laici, decretis canonis resistentes, ecclesias violentes tenere praesumpserint, ipsi excommunicentur; in ecclesiis vero illis nullum divinum officium fiat, nullus ibi oret, lumen non ponatur, mortuus non sepeliatur." [66]

It might be argued that Bishop Ivo of Chartres (1090–1116) considered the interdict as a new and unusual measure of discipline. Thus, Ferraris [67] employs the phrase of Ivo *"remedium insolitum ob suam nimirum novitatem"* to prove that the interdict has a very late origin. But Kober [68] contends that this phrase arouses suspicion when it is recalled that Ivo was one of the foremost canonists of his time; consequently such a statement could scarcely have emanated from him. Moreover, Crnica [69] affirms that the great Bishop of Chartres clearly distinguished between *excommunication* and *interdicts.* Such expressions as *interdicere ecclesiasticum ministerium, terra interdicatur, interdictio,* frequently appear from the beginning of the twelfth century, and it seems to be from that time that the term *interdict* assumed its present technical meaning.[70]

Towards the end of the twelfth century the interdict had such great and effective application that it suffices merely to mention the great interdicts which were imposed during that period. Thus, an interdict was laid on Scotland in the year 1180 by Pope Alexander III.[71] Likewise, very severe interdicts were laid on France in the year 1200, and on England in the year 1208 by Pope Innocent III.[72] These great national disasters are so well known and recognized by all as types of the interdict in its full development, that there is little need to expatiate further concerning them.

---

[66] Mansi, 20, 498.

[67] *Prompta Bibliotheca Canonica,* "Interdictum," art. I, n. 36.

[68] *Op. cit.,* XXI, 18.

[69] *Op. cit.,* p. 142.

[70] Cf. *Conc. Lateran,* I (1123), c. 11, Mansi, 21, 284.

[71] *Ep.* XVII, ad. reg.—Hardouin, VI, 1422.

[72] Krehbiel, *The Interdict,* p. 110 ff.

It is also a recognized fact that in the thirteenth century the interdict was applied more frequently, and scarcely a Synod can be found which does not in some way or other make mention of the interdict.[73]

Upon what fundamental principle was the interdict built? Fundamentally, the interdict seems to have its origin and development from the penalty of excommunication which comes down from the time of the Apostles. It seems both natural and reasonable that this punishment of excommunication should be extended to punish not only the guilty party of a given crime but also his accessories.

It must be remembered, however, that this radical change in the disciplinary system of the Church did not immediately meet with the approval of all ecclesiastical authorities. In many cases the stand of leading ecclesiastics was strong against the idea of general excommunication.[74] Thus, it happened during the controversy concerning the date of celebrating Easter, that Pope Victor excommunicated the Church of Asia, but Eusebius relates that the other bishops, displeased with the stern policy of Victor, chided him "to consider the things of peace, of neighborly union and love."[75] Another instance of general excommunication is shown in the case of Classicianus, a Roman official who, with his whole family, was excommunicated by Bishop Auxilius for seizing an offender while seeking refuge at the altar. In this case, Saint Augustine, upon being asked to intercede, firmly opposed such extension of the censure. The great Doctor said he would be glad to know on what grounds Auxilius could defend himself for condemning the wife and members of the family for the sins of the head of the family. Addressing himself to Auxilius, Saint Augustine wrote: "...Atque hinc venerationem tuam ita sibi succensuisse, ut ecclesiasticorum confectione gestorum cum omni domo sua anathematis sententia feriretur."[76] In the same epistle he relates that other bishops made use

[73] Kober, *op. cit.*, XXI, 20.

[74] Howland, *The Interdict, A. H. A. Report*, 1899, I, 433.

[75] Eusebius, *History*, V, 24—*MPL*, 20, 498.

[76] *Ep.* CCL ad Auxilium—*MPL*, 33, 1066.

of the same disciplinary measure. Thus, he writes: "Audisti fortasse aliquos magni nominis sacerdotes cum domo sua quempiam anathemasse peccantium? Sed forte si essent interrogati, reperirentur idonei reddere inde rationem."[77] Hence it can readily be seen that the extension of the penalty of excommunication was condemned in the most severe terms by Saint Augustine. Such opposition on the part of so great an ecclesiastic as Saint Augustine only serves to explain that the interdict had a very gradual development, and that only after its necessity was apparent did it receive full recognition.

Furthermore, the spirit of Roman Law was opposed to the idea of punishing the innocent; and while this law retained its grasp on the minds of the people, a censure of the character of general excommunication or interdict could flourish but little. But the decline of Roman Law made general excommunication possible, and the necessity of the Church in those days demanded it. However, besides the decline of Roman Law and the necessity of the Church, the growth of general excommunication was due in a large measure to the advent of the Teutons, whose ideals and traditions favored such extension of punishments. Thus, according to the Teutonic mind, the clan was to a certain degree responsible for the conduct of the individual, an idea which was naturally sympathetic with a censure punishing many for the act of one guilty member. The natural result, therefore, was the rapid spread of general excommunication from Roman lands to the territories of the Teutons, a fact which was calculated to make general excommunication the most powerful and efficient weapon of the Church.[78]

But seemingly, at least, general excommunication was a weapon entirely too severe. As has been stated before, excommunication (of the individual) is the most severe of all ecclesiastical punishments; for it separates the delinquent entirely from all association with his fellow-Christians, besides depriving him of the use of the Sacraments. Now, when such a punishment was extended so as to involve even

---

[77] *Ibidem.*

[78] Krehbiel, *The Interdict*, p. 6.

innocent persons, it was but natural that the more prudent prelates realized that it was calculated, in many cases at least, to do more harm than good. On the other hand, there were many, especially among the lower clergy, who were very reluctant to surrender a weapon so powerful, and the natural result was a moderation of general excommunication to the less severe penalty of the interdict.[79] This change, however, was very slow and gradual, as might well be imagined, when one remembers how certain prelates favored the relaxation and even the abolition of general excommunication, while others fought to retain it in its full severity. It is for this reason, therefore, that it is so difficult to ascertain exactly when the first interdict, as it is now understood, was imposed.

It seems necessary at this point to study the character of this censure, with a view of discerning exactly in what respects it essentially differs from general excommunication. The first great difference lies in the fact that those under interdict were not separated from the communion of the faithful; furthermore, in most cases of interdict, some services were permitted. Of course, the interdict, from its beginning until it received full ecclesiastical recognition, was under the control of the bishops in their respective territories. Moreover, the effectiveness of the interdict increased in proportion as the power of the Papacy increased.[80]

So closely has the interdict been identified with other penalties, that it is not an easy task to determine exactly when the term was first employed in its present technical meaning. In fact, cases are recorded in the sources as excommunication which, in all probability, were interdict. Thus, mention is made of the interdict in a canon of Pope Innocent III (1198–1216), wherein he describes it as a *cessatio a divinorum celebratione*. The following is part of the canon:

> Cum civitas Parmensis et cives ejus excommunicatione subjecti fuissent.... Volumus autem ut a praedictis

[79] Krehbiel, *Ibidem*.
[80] Krehbiel, *Ibidem*.

> canonicis sufficienti prius cautione recepta quod debeant parere justitiae coram vobis, interdictum, appellatione praeposita, relaxetis. Si vero latae sententiae parere noluerint, eos per excommunicationis sententiam compellatis.[81]

Judging from the various documents in which the term *interdict* appears, one is forced to conclude that even until late in the twelfth century, the term had a very loose and wide meaning.

According to Kober[82] the identification of the interdict with excommunication consisted more in the technical expression than upon likeness of character. It is a known fact that the interdict differed from excommunication in essence and contents. Thus, excommunication was always regarded as an interior mode of punishment, touching the individual and separating him from communion with the faithful; it likewise deprived one of all the spiritual benefits concomitant with membership in the Church. The interdict, on the other hand, did not suspend the interior connection with the ecclesiastical communion, but only curtailed the external functions. In other words, when an individual was excommunicated, exclusion from worship was a consequence or an effect of his penalty; but when in the question of interdict, the exclusion from worship was the very essence of the penalty. Hence, when the faithful in general were forbidden to associate with an excommunicated person, it was because such a person, excluded as he was from the Church, was looked upon as a heathen and a publican. The matter was quite different, however, when there was question of an interdicted person, who did not cease to be united with the communion of the faithful; therefore there was no obligation on the part of the faithful to shun him.[83]

From what has been said in the immediately preceding paragraph, it would appear that according to its character and contents, the interdict was a far lesser evil than ex-

---

[81] Innocent, III, *Ep.* 403,—*MPL,* 214, 378.
[82] *Op. cit.,* XXI, 22.
[83] Kober, *op. cit.,* XXI, 23.

communication; nevertheless, it was a very severe and dreadful punishment, often inflicted upon entire congregations, cities and nations. Now when a penalty such as a local interdict is extended so as to affect an entire nation, it is difficult to imagine any greater calamity. Frequently the interdict consisted in the cessation of all sacred functions.[84] It is true, nevertheless, that all the interdicts did not contain exactly the same prohibitions and provisions. "Vere dicere non possumus, omnia interdicta eosdem effectus produxisse, in genere tamen affirmare debemus, omnia quae ad cultum divinum pertinent paucis rebus tantum exceptis, fuisse prohibita, prout id speciatim apparet ex interdictis saeculo XIII occurrentibus, et praesertim ex mitigationibus eodem saeculo legislatione communi introductis." [85] The different prohibitions of the various interdicts are often apparent from the different terms by which they were represented. Thus, the interdict has been called a "closing of the churches," a "rescinding of all holy functions" and the like.[86] The Council of Toledo, in the year 683, makes use of the expression "subducere divinae servitutis cultum;" it also mentions the cessation of "divina consueta" and the "oblatio singularis sacrificii." [87]

The interdict pronounced on his diocese by Hincmar of Laon is an excellent example of the effects of a local interdict in its strictest form. Mention of this interdict has already been made; it will be remembered that, according to this extreme measure, every divine function was absolutely forbidden. It can readily be seen that the various interdicts had different effects as to their number, kind and severity. It was but natural that an interdict would be more faithfully observed in one locality than in another; moreover, certain interdicts contained such drastic measures that they could not always be enforced. "Duri vere semper populo Christiano effectus interdicti fuerunt, ideoque semper et ubique summum dolorem summamque tristi-

[84] Kober, *Ibidem.*

[85] Crnica, *op. cit.*, p. 143.

[86] Kober, *op. cit.*, XXI, 20.

[87] C. VII, Mansi, 11, 1069.

tiam produxerunt, ablatio vero interdicti econtra indescriptible gaudium et laetitiam." [88]

Just as Hincmar of Rheims reprehended his nephew, Hincmar of Laon, because of his extreme severity in forbidding Baptism to infants, and even Viaticum to the dying, so the later councils endeavored to set up legislation whereby such sacraments as were absolutely necessary could not be forbidden during the time of an interdict. The Council of Limoges, in the year 1031, despite its strict and drastic measures, permitted the silent worship behind closed doors, Baptism and the Sacraments of the dying: "Divinum officium per omnes ecclesias latenter agatur et baptismus petentibus tribuatur....Poenitentia et viaticum in exitu mortis tribuatur." [89] Pope Alexander III permitted the celebration of divine services, and allowed the administration of Baptism to infants and Penance to the dying.[90]

Although it was the severity of the interdict which brought about the desired result, nevertheless, it cannot be denied that interdicts very frequently were the indirect cause of lowering the moral standards of the people. It was, no doubt, the realization of this fact that prompted the ecclesiastical authorities to modify the rigor of this disciplinary measure. Thus, Crnica writes: "...*interdictum tamen non raro indirecte etiam corruptionem in populo Christiano produxit. Nam populus divinis officiis, sacramentis, praedicatione verbi Dei, frequentatione ecclesiarum, orationibus publicis, aliisque consolationibus fidei, quae quasi unica sunt emolumenta ad fidem et bonos mores servandos, privatus, quasi necessario debuit non tantum in moribus relaxari, verum etiam in fide frigescere; unde tam haereses quam alia mala in populo creverunt, praesertim cum interdicta non raro nimis longe duraverint.*" [91]

The condition of affairs can be understood when one considers that churches were closed, bells were silent, public worship was stopped, and the people were denied all the

---

[88] Crnica, *op. cit.*, p. 144.

[89] Mansi, 19, 541.

[90] C. 11, X *de sponsal*, IV, 1.

[91] *Op. cit.*, p. 144.

consolations of Religion save such as were absolutely necessary. Moreover, when one considers the ardent religious spirit which prevailed among the people of those days, and the interior love with which they felt themselves attracted to worship God, it was not to be wondered at that they looked upon an interdict as the most severe and most dreadful calamity which could befall any nation. The great sorrow which an interdict caused the faithful in general, may be measured by the great joy which they experienced when it was raised. It is related that the Cardinal legate Octavian, whom Pope Innocent III had sent to France to raise the interdict, had scarcely arrived when he was received by the people as a messenger from heaven bringing salvation and peace. He was acclaimed by all of high and low station alike. They all saw in his coming an end to the period of sorrow and distress, and when the interdict had at last been removed, the hearts of all were full of joy and gratitude.[92]

Section V.—The Immediate Purpose of the Interdict

Having seen how the interdict came into existence, it will not be amiss to consider briefly the various theories advanced concerning its immediate purpose. Some argue that the interdict was generally imposed for the purpose of showing displeasure and disapproval towards public misconduct. Others contend that the interdict was sometimes intended to propitiate a Saint offended because of some insult towards his relics.[93] This latter theory, however, is difficult to support; thus, Krehbiel[94] objects to it on the grounds that the propitiation of saints is never mentioned in the sentence as the purpose of the interdict. Another theory difficult to support is that the interdict was often imposed with a view of warning the faithful against future transgressions; for in all the cases mentioned, the interdict was inflicted only after the transgression had been

---

[92] Kober, *op. cit.*, p. 28.

[93] Hinschius, *System des Katholischen Kirchenrechts*, IV, 806.

[94] *The Interdict*, p. 10.

committed. The famous interdict which Hincmar of Laon inflicted on his diocese does seem different in purpose to all others; certainly this sentence of interdict was not inflicted as a punishment. Evidently the troubled bishop inflicted the severe measure of discipline upon his diocese with a view of creating popular opinion in his own favor, and thereby bring about his reinstatement.

There is reason to believe that the interdict was often imposed as a medicinal penalty *(poena medicinalis)*, i.e., to improve the spiritual health of the delinquent. Moreover, the interdict was sometimes imposed as a punishment, i.e., a vindictive penalty. That this was the sole purpose of the interdict, seems to be the opinion of Hinschius.[95] This opinion of Hinschius, however, is questioned by Krehbiel [96] for the reason that in many cases offenders were obliged to fulfill long and severe penances even after the interdict was removed.

The immediate purpose of each individual interdict can often be determined from the wording of the sentence of the judge who imposed it. Thus, in a letter of Pope Innocent III, in which the great Pontiff rebuked the Templars for not observing interdicts, direct mention is made of a *medicinal penalty: "Templi suis beneficiis fovere non desinit, maculam impingere non verentes, audeant publice praedicare quod per Apostolicae Sedis indulta cujuscumque civitatis interdictae vel oppidi omnes ecclesiae successive in eorum jucundo adventu debeant aperiri, et ibidem divina officia celebrari, prout eis nunc in ista, nunc in alia videbitur expedire, non attendentes quod ex praesumptione hujusmodi contemnitur medicinalis poena medela, imo quasi penitus enervatur."* [97]

In determining the purpose of the interdict, one must bear in mind that the paramount question was to deal out justice and to defend righteousness without respect of persons, to curb the defiance of powerful lords who did violence to the Church and to society in general. When it is remem-

[95] *Op. cit.*, IV, 747-748.

[96] *Op. cit.*, p. 11.

[97] Innocent III, *Ep.* 121,—*MPL*, 215, 1217-1218.

bered that such offenders turned deaf ears to the admonitions of the Church, and derided her threats, there is little room for surprise when the Church was forced to adopt the drastic means of depriving the people of public worship. Kober [98] makes the statement that what could not be accomplished through charity and the love of God in obstinate offenders, was accomplished only by means of disciplinary measures as severe as the interdict. Moreover, it must be borne in mind that when the offenders were powerful rulers, as was frequently the case, there was the additional evil of scandal; for if kings and princes could set at naught all the principles of decency and morality, their bad example would, without doubt, lower the moral tone of the people.

The interdict with all its severity stands vindicated when it is remembered that in nearly every case the purpose of the interdict was fulfilled.[99]

The interdict has been called a compulsion in the form of passive resistance, i.e., the Church authorities, by suspending divine services in a given district, created such high feeling and popular opinion against offenders, who in many instances were headstrong rulers, that submission to the demands of the Church was the only solution for their difficult problems. Indeed, if one considers the condition of affairs during medieval times, he can readily understand that the interdict was a necessary and sometimes the only means of protecting society against the terrible effects resulting from the scandalous conduct of certain unscrupulous secular rulers. Moreover, it is difficult to imagine to what excesses certain kings and princes might have gone, and to what a low ebb religious life might have fallen, if the Church had had no means of enforcing her mandates.

To the popular objection that the interdict was unjust and unreasonable because it caused the innocent to suffer with the guilty, it may be urged that ultimately the interdict was for the protection of the innocent, since its frequent aim was to compel unruly potentates to comply to the dic-

98 "*Das Interdikt*," *AkKR*, XXI, 29.

99 Kober, *op. cit.*, XXI, 29.

tates of decency and morality. It must be admitted even by the enemies of the interdict that no greater hardship could befall the innocent than the reign of license and lawlessness which certainly would have resulted had not the crimes of the guilty been checked by so efficient a means. Certainly the Church was not anxious to impose interdicts, because she realized, as no one else could realize, the hardships which they wrought on the innocent. Consequently, the Church permitted the innocent to suffer only to subdue a greater evil. Although the measures of the various interdicts seem rather drastic, it can safely be asserted that the purpose which the interdict served was even greater.

Notwithstanding all that has been said in justification of the interdict, it was, nevertheless, considered a punishment too severe, and consequently, numerous complaints were made against it. The question arose as to whether in its workings it furthered the religious and moral life of the people. The interdict was considered an injustice not only to the people but also to the clergy, because it affected them as well, depriving them of their property and freedom and even endangering their lives.[100] But the Church in punishing those not guilty, certainly could find justification in Holy Writ; for the cities of Sodom and Gomorrha were destroyed and all the inhabitants thereof; "And He destroyed these cities, and all the country about, and all the inhabitants of the cities."[101] In like manner the practice of the Church is supported by that portion of the Scriptures which narrate the promulgation of the Ten Commandments: "...I am the Lord the God, mighty, jealous, visiting the iniquity of the fathers upon the children, unto the third and fourth generation of them that hate Me."[102] Indeed, when all the facts are considered, it is not so difficult to understand why the Church felt justified in allowing the innocent to suffer with the guilty.

In this connection, it will not be amiss to consider briefly one concrete case: Oderic Vitalis describes the conditions

---

[100] Kober, *op. cit.*, XXI, 31.

[101] *Genesis*, XIX, 25.

[102] *Exodus*, XX, 5.

in Normandy under Duke Robert in the following terms: "Provincia tota erat dissoluta et praedones catervatim discurrebant per vicos et per rura nimiumque super inermes debacchabatur latrociniorum caterva." [103] It is the opinion of Kober [104] that this description can be applied with equal force to other countries. He further remarks that it was the innocent and defenseless who suffered on account of these detestable outrages without being able to offer resistance. It was, therefore, with a view of ultimately defending the innocent that the Church permitted them to suffer with the guilty. The Church could scarcely avoid the temporary evil of allowing the innocent to suffer when it was her purpose to combat barbarity and wickedness, and eventually bring about peace and happiness to the same innocent persons upon whom the interdict weighed so heavily.

Section VI.—Modification of the Interdict

Since the interdict was a modified form of general excommunication, it is but natural that interdicts of earlier times were in many respects more stringent and severe than those of subsequent centuries. Thus, in general, the local interdict deprived the district affected by it of some or all of the following: Divine services, the sacraments and canonical burial.[105] The divine services included the canonical hours, sacraments, and in general, any ecclesiastical function which can be performed only by a priest. In fact, even the Mass, the centre of Catholic worship, was permitted only with certain limitations and under certain conditions. Hence, even after Pope Innocent III permitted the celebration of Mass to provide Holy Viaticum for the dying, the ringing of bells, admittance of excommunicated or interdicted persons and chanting was strictly forbidden. The service was always conducted behind closed doors, and the prayers were recited in a low tone of voice. The com-

[103] Bouquet, *Recueil des Historiens des Gaules et de la France*, t. XII, p. 630.

[104] *Op. cit.*, XXI, 35.

[105] Krehbiel, *The Interdict*, p. 13.

mon recitation of the divine office (canonical hours) was forbidden in time of interdict, and consequently, each cleric recited his office in private.

The different circumstances of time and place, however, soon affected various changes and modifications of the original regulations. Thus, in the year 1203, it happened that Stephen, Bishop of Tournay, wrote to the Archbishop of Rheims, with a view of preventing another interdict from being inflicted upon Flanders. In his epistle, he stated that the wounds resulting from a former interdict were still bleeding, and if a second blow followed moral death would ensue, and the heresies which had already begun would take new root.[106] In like manner, the Bishop of Bergamo together with his clergy, described to Pope Innocent III the results of the interdict which had been imposed upon the city. Pope Boniface VIII certainly recognized the same dire results of the interdict when he wrote: "Quia vero ex districtione hujusmodi statutorum excrescit indevotio populi, pululant haereses, et infinita pericula animarum insurgunt, ac ecclesiis sine culpa earum debita obsequia subtrahuntur..." [107]

It was with a view of removing or lessening these evils that the Church set about to mitigate the rigor of the interdict, and thereby lighten the burden upon the people. Originally the interdict consisted in the cessation of all ecclesiastical functions.[108] It is admitted, however, that Baptism and Penance (to the dying) were nearly always exceptions from the general prohibition.[109] In the year 1209, Pope Innocent III made an additional exception in permitting the administration of Confirmation.[110]

Concerning the Sacrament of Matrimony, it may be said that it was not generally forbidden during the time of an interdict; the reason probably rests in the fact that the contracting parties, themselves, are the ministers of this

---

[106] Crnica, *op. cit.*, p. 144; Kober, *op. cit.*, XXI, 37.

[107] C. 24, *de sent. excom.*, V, 11 in VI°.

[108] Kober, *op. cit.*, XXI, 39.

[109] Crnica, *op. cit.*, p. 145.

[110] C. 43, X, *de sent. excom.*, V, 39.

Sacrament. In a few cases, however, it was expressly forbidden.[111]

While an interdict was in force, ecclesiastical burial was generally forbidden.[112] From this general prohibition, however, exception was made in favor of clerics, beggars, strangers and children under two years of age.[113] When an interdict was imposed upon Vendome, Ivo of Chartres exempted only clerics and paupers from the general rule denying ecclesiastical burial.[114] The severity of this measure soon moderated, and a method was adopted whereby laymen were denied burial only in consecrated ground. It must be remembered that the concessions granted by Pope Boniface VIII, by virtue of which divine services could be celebrated on certain great feasts, did not include the right to bury the dead on such feasts. The reason for this distinction is clear when it is recalled that burial was not considered as a part of the *officia divina.*[115]

The reign of Pope Boniface VIII marked an epoch in the history of the interdict; for it was during the reign of this great Pontiff that the greatest changes took place towards the relaxation of severity of this disciplinary measure. Accordingly, in his celebrated decretal *Alma,* many concessions were granted.[116] Thus, during a general local interdict, permission was given to celebrate Mass and other divine functions with all the usual solemnities on the great feasts of Christmas, Easter, Pentecost, the Assumption of the Blessed Virgin, and the feast of Corpus Christi. Of course, ecclesiastics, whether secular or regular, could not avail themselves of the concessions just mentioned if they, themselves, were bound by *personal interdict,* nor could they do so in the case of *particular local interdict,* i.e., when a church, for example, is placed under a local interdict. Nor did these concessions obtain in the case of a *general*

111 Du Cange, *Glossar.*, art. "Interdictum," VI, 1486.

112 Krehbiel, *op. cit.*, p. 17.

113 Du Cange, *Glossar.*, art. "Interdictum," VI, 1486.

114 Du Cange, *Ibidem.*

115 C. 3, X, *de priv.*, V, 33.

116 C. 24, *de sent. excom.*, V, 11, in VI°.

personal interdict. Consequently, these concessions obtained only in the case of a *general local interdict.*[117]

Furthermore, those who by their crimes caused a general local interdict to be imposed, were explicitly excluded by Pope Boniface VIII, in the same decretal *Alma,* from the privilege of either celebrating or assisting at divine services. The reason for this last stipulation is that such persons automatically incurred a *personal interdict,* and therefore, could not celebrate or assist at divine services in any place whatever, even in a place not under interdict.[118]

In a canon of Pope Innocent III, regulations are given regarding the recitation of the canonical hours in conventual churches; accordingly, it was decreed that clerics were permitted to read the hours in a low tone of voice, so that they could not be heard outside of the building; moreover, the hours could not be chanted; the doors of the church must remain closed during the recitation, and excommunicated and interdicted persons were to be strictly excluded. The importance of this canon is such that it will not be amiss to quote it in its exact wording:

> In illo enim verbo, per quod paenitentiam morientibus non negatur, viaticum etiam, quod vere paenitentibus exhibetur, intelligi volumus, ut nec ipsum etiam decedentibus denegetur. Licet autem per generale interdictum denegetur omnibus tam unctio quam ecclesiastica sepultura, ut clerici decedentes, qui tamen servaverint interdictum, in coemeterio ecclesiae sine campanarum pulsatione, cessantibus solemnitatibus omnibus, cum silentio tumulentur. Et in conventualibus ecclesiis bini et bini, vel simul tres, horas canonicas valeant legere, non cantare, januis clausis, interdictis et excommunicatis exclusis, et voce ita demissa, quod exterius audire non possunt; quum et regularibus secundum privilegium, sedis apostolicae sit indultum, ut, quum generale interdictum terrae fuerit, liceat eis, januis clausis, excommunicatis et interdictis exclusis, non pulsatis campanis, suppressa voce celebrare divina.

---

117 Smith, *op. cit.,* n. 3342.

118 C. 16, *de sent. excom.,* V, 11, in VI°.

> Recipientibus autem signum crucis non negamus, quo minus eis ob reverentiam crucifixi paenitentia, quum postulaverint, injungatur, quod et aliis peregrinis potest miseridorditer indulgeri.[119]

Pope Gregory IX later permitted priests, under the conditions mentioned in the above canon of Pope Innocent III to celebrate Mass once a week to provide Holy Viaticum for the dying.[120] Kober,[121] however, points out that this mitigation is of older date, since it was the necessary consequence of the concession granted by Pope Innocent III, whereby Holy Viaticum was permitted to the dying.

Pope Boniface VIII made a further concession in allowing the administration of Confirmation not only to children but also to adults; the same Pontiff also provided for the consecration of the Chrism on Holy Thursday.[122]

The later Popes really made no new concessions, but simply developed those made by Pope Boniface VIII; in other words, they extended these concessions to certain other feasts. At first, only the feasts of Christmas, Easter, Pentecost and the Assumption of the Blessed Virgin were included in the privilege granted by Pope Boniface VIII, whereby these feasts could be celebrated with full solemnity. Later, Pope Martin V, in 1429, extended the privilege to include the feast of Corpus Christi.[123] Finally, Pope Eugene IV, in his constitution "Excellentissimum" of May 26, 1431, extended the privilege to the whole octave of the feast of Corpus Christi.[124]

In later times many favors were granted to the Religious Orders, by virtue of which they were exempt from the jurisdiction of the bishops in the matter of interdicts, and, consequently, could be interdicted by the Pope only.[125]

The people naturally experienced much relief in the privileges granted to the various Religious Orders, because they

---

119 C. 11, X, *de paenit.*, V, 38.
120 C. 57, X, *de poenit.*, V, 38.
121 *Op. cit.*, XXI, 40.
122 C. 19, *de sent. excom.*, V, 11, in VI°.
123 Const. "*Ineffabile*," May 26, 1429—*Bullar. Rom.*, IV, 732.
124 *Fontes*, n. 48.
125 Kober, *op. cit.*, XXI, 43.

were thereby given an unusual opportunity of attending Mass and other divine functions during the time of an interdict.

Section VII.—Manner of Imposing an Interdict

According to the pre-Code discipline there were two ways in which an interdict could be incurred: (a) that which *ipso facto* or automatically followed the commission of certain delicts, and this was known as a *latae sententiae penalty;* (b) that which followed the sentence of an ecclesiastical judge, and interdicts of this type were called *ferendae sententiae* penalties.[126] This provision of law is still retained by the Code.[127] In pre-Code times, as now, an interdict was incurred *latae sententiae* only in the case of some very unusual offense, for example, the murder of a cardinal, or the refusal on the part of a prince to receive Papal legates into his kingdom.[128] Furthermore, an entire city might fall under the same sentence, if it in any way aided in the murder of a cardinal, or failed to punish the guilty party within the space of one month.[129] Likewise, magistrates who demanded or collected taxes from churches incurred an interdict *latae sententiae.*[130] A similar sentence was also incurred if the officials of any city in which a Pope died, in any way hindered the execution of the laws established by the various Councils for Papal elections.[131]

An interdict *ferendae sententiae* could be imposed only by those having jurisdiction in the contentious forum.[132] Thus, any superior who could impose a sentence of excommunication or suspension, could also impose an interdict. Hence, the Pope's power to impose interdicts extended over the whole Church, while the power of bishops, with few exceptions, was limited to their respective terri-

---

[126] Krehbiel, *The Interdict*, p. 19.

[127] Can. 2217, §1, n. 2.

[128] C. Unic. *de consuet.*, I, 1, Extravag. comm.

[129] C. 5, *de poenit.*, V, 9, in VI°.

[130] C. 4, *de censuris*, III, 20, in VI°.

[131] C. 3, *de elect.*, I, 6, in VI°.

[132] Smith, *op. cit.*, n. 3346.

tories. A singular exception was the favor granted by Pope Innocent III to Conrad, Bishop of Metz, whereby the authority of Conrad to inflict censures against malefactors of the Church was extended to any diocese, provided the resident bishop failed to take action against the offenders.[133] Krehbiel,[134] however, points out that this power was delegated and not strictly ordinary. An Archbishop's power to lay interdicts was limited to the confines of his own province; prior to the Council of Trent, however, an Archbishop could declare a personal interdict against one of his suffragan bishops,[135] but the Tridentine Council took this power from the Archbishops and reserved it to the Roman Pontiff.[136] There was a provision of law which required bishops to consult their Chapters before imposing an interdict;[137] it seems, however, that a custom to the contrary abrogated this law.[138] It occasionally happened that bishops sought the confirmation of the Pope, in order that their interdicts, reinforced by papal approbation, might be more readily enforced and obeyed. The sources show that many interdicts were declared by Provincial Councils, while the interdicts imposed by General Councils were more rare.[139]

As the power of the Church grew, many ecclesiastical superiors began to impose interdicts by reason of the office they held. Thus, before the Tridentine Council, legates and nuncios of the Pope enjoyed almost unlimited power in the matter of imposing interdicts.[140]

It was the prerogative of cardinals to interdict the churches, the titles of which they bore.[141] It was generally agreed that priests could not impose interdicts; the few instances in which they may appear to have done so can be explained by the fact that special authorization of the Ordinary was given to such priests.

---

[133] Innocent, III, *Ep.* 187,—*MPL,* 216, 709.
[134] *Op. cit.,* p. 21.
[135] C. 52, X, *de sent. excom.* V, 39.
[136] Sess. XIII, *de ref.,* c. 8.
[137] C. 1, X, *de excess.,* V, 31.
[138] Krehbiel, *op. cit.,* p. 22.
[139] C. 2, Mansi, 22, 9; Hefele. *Conciliengeschichte,* IV, 792.
[140] Krehbiel, *Ibidem.*
[141] Kober, *op. cit.,* XXII, 8.

There were two conditions under which a Chapter might impose an interdict. The first condition was that they must have independent jurisdiction over the property which they held; accordingly, in the event of offenses touching these possessions, the Chapter imposed interdicts.[142] The second condition was in the event of vacancy of the Episcopal See, the Chapter exercised the authority of the Bishop, and, consequently, imposed interdicts. In the course of time, Chapters lost this power to impose interdicts during the vacancy of the See, for it was the ruling of the Council of Trent [143] that within eight days after the death of the Bishop, a vicar should be elected to perform the functions of the Bishop until a successor should be appointed. Hence, only the vicar capitular could declare interdicts during the vacancy of the Episcopal See.

It appears that the Inquisition had the authority to inflict interdicts. Thus, Vacandard [144] states that the leading canonists and theologians of that period approved the strictest penalties inflicted by the Inquisition. He further states that Saint Raymond of Pennafort, a counsellor of Pope Gregory IX, defended the penalty of excommunication of heretics and schismatics, their banishment and the confiscation of their property. Lea,[145] commenting on the Bull "Ad Extirpanda" of Pope Innocent IV, writes that Pope Clement IV, in 1265, revised this Bull, making some necessary changes, principally adding the word "Inquisitors." Lea argues from this that the Inquisition had become a recognized instrument in the prosecution of heresy. He further states that Pope Clement IV, in 1266, repeated the order of Pope Innocent IV to the Inquisitors to enforce the legislation with free use of excommunication and *interdict*. In this connection, Vacandard [146] points out that the Church, in the person of the Popes, used every means possible, especially excommunication, to compel the State to punish heretics. Although Vacandard makes no express mention

142 C. 5, X, *de consuet.*, I, 4.

143 Sess. XXIV, *de ref.*, c. 16.

144 *The Inquisition*, p. 123.

145 *The Inquisition in Spain*, I, 339.

146 *The Inquisition*, p. 105.

of the interdict, it is quite probable that the Church employed this measure against passive civil officials, especially since the interdict was often the only means the Church possessed of forcing the State authorities to comply with her demands.

It is to be further noted that before a sentence of interdict could be duly imposed, the formalities of warning and citation must be observed. The reason for such warning was twofold. In the first place, a warning was given because the interdict was the last resort, hence, it was the intention of the Church authorities to give the offender a final chance to submit; the second reason for the warning was that the interdict sometimes wrought harm on the Church itself, and, consequently, was to be imposed only when all other means had failed.[147]

It was frequently stipulated in these warnings exactly when the sentence of interdict would become effective. This was sometimes done by naming some exact date in the calendar on which date the delinquent's period of grace would expire, or by setting an arbitrary number of days of grace. The different periods of grace varied much as to their duration. Thus one instance is given in which the period of grace lasted three days: "Si autem a die denuntiationis captivatum cum satisfactione infra triduum non restituerit, terra ipsorum supponatur interdicto." [148] In another instance the period of grace lasted two months: "Et sic per duos menses nisi ad satisfactionem pervenerint, expectentur, quibus elapsis, castra ipsorum supponantur interdicto.[149]

If a warning went unheeded, *citation* was to follow. Thus, the offender was summoned to appear before an authorized superior, before whom he should state the reasons why the interdict should not be imposed, and also to state the reasons why he did not heed the warning.[150] It is likely that a king or prince was rarely summoned for the purpose of

[147] Kober, *op. cit.*, XXII, 29; Krehbiel, *op. cit.*, p. 37.

[148] Conc. Trev. (1238), C. 5, Mansi, 23, 480.

[149] Conc. Campanic. (1238), C. 17, Mansi, 23, 491.

[150] Krehbiel, *op. cit.*, p. 39.

citation, because the crimes of such a person were generally so well known that there could be little reason to doubt the truth of the charge.

After the warning and citation, it was necessary that the interdict be promulgated. For this promulgation there was no fixed formula; the one requisite was that the form employed must be explicit and easy of perception. It soon became the custom to put the sentence in writing, and, if possible, read it to the offending party. Later, it became a fairly common practice in making promulgation, to state explicitly the reasons for the interdict; moreover, the judge frequently gave an authentic copy of the sentence to the person or persons about to be interdicted.[151]

Although there was no authentic or fixed formula to be employed in the promulgation of an interdict, nevertheless, a rather common practice soon developed. In other words, although the actual wording of different formulae varied considerably, the general character and meaning of various formulae were quite the same.[152] Accordingly, in nearly every formula, mention was made concerning the causes of the interdict, the services that were prohibited, and, in some cases, how long the sentence was to last. Moreover, penalties were sometimes prescribed for those who refused to observe the sentence.[153] It was not at all unlikely that some of the more important interdicts were promulgated with great solemnity. Thus, Hurter [153a] gives a very dramatic description of the promulgation of the interdict in France in 1199; he relates how the Papal legate, vested in purple, read the sentence of interdict in the Cathedral Church in the presence of eighteen bishops and a great number of abbots, priests and people.

After the promulgation of the interdict, another publication or legal notice followed, which enabled the people to know that they were under interdict.[154] This publication was generally made by reading the sentence of interdict

[151] Krehbiel, *op. cit.*, p. 39.
[152] De Cange, *Glossar.*, art. "Interdictum," VI, 1486.
[153] Du Cange, *Ibidem.*
[153a] *Storia d'Innocenzo III*, IV, 415.
[154] Conc. Arelat. (1275), C. 5, Hardouin, 8, 728.

in church during public services, or by posting it in some public place. According to a regulation contained in the Constitution "Ad Evitanda" of Pope Martin V, this publication was necessary whether the interdict was *latae* or *ferendae sententiae.*[155]

It would be a great mistake to suppose that it was always an easy matter to make this publication; for certain secular rulers did all in their power to prevent the sentence of interdict from being published in their respective countries. Thus, Henry II, in 1170, forbade entrance to England to any messenger bearing notice of an interdict.[156] Without such publication the people could not be expected to know that they were under interdict, and, much less, could they be expected to observe it. The fact that publication was prohibited, or even unlawfully impeded, did not alter the matter, because it was the accepted rule of the Church itself that the interdict must be published if the sentence was to be valid.

It is clear, therefore, that the Church took all possible care to give offenders a final chance to submit; consequently, no one could plead ignorance either of his crime or of the sentence of interdict. It must also be remembered that anyone about to be interdicted had the right of appeal to Rome. If such appeal were made before an interdict was promulgated, no sentence of interdict could be made until the Holy See had given an answer to the appeal; for it was a ruling of Pope Innocent III that any sentence of interdict laid after appeal should be null and void.[157] It sometimes happened, however, that the right of appeal was denied by special order.[158] If the appeal were made after the publication of the sentence, it did not suspend the sentence, hence the interdict had to be observed while the Holy See considered the appeal.[159]

The length of duration of interdicts varied considerably according to the circumstances. Thus, the importance and

155 *Fontes,* n. 45.
156 Krehbiel, *op. cit.,* p. 40.
157 Innocent III, *Ep.* 368,—*MPL,* 214, 351.
158 Innocent III, *Ep.* 200,—*MPL,* 214, 249.
159 Krehbiel, *op. cit.,* p. 42.

standing of the offender, and the enormity of the offense had much to do in prolonging the duration. In general, it may be said that interdicts remained in force until their end was accomplished. In one instance the interdict was in force so long that the people lost all relish for religious services; for in a gloss of the decretal *Alma,* it is related that an interdict lasted for thirty years in a city in the province of Ancona.[160] The natural result of this interdict was that persons thirty and forty years old, never having heard or seen Mass celebrated, and others having lost all interest in their Religion, derided the priests as they resumed the services.

The interdict imposed by Alexander IV on Portugal lasted for twelve years.[161] Another interdict inflicted by Pope Gregory IX on Sicily lasted for sixty years.[162] Of course, the cases just cited were extreme and exceptional. On making a careful examination of the cases available, one will find that the average duration of an interdict was about two years.[163]

Although all persons residing in the district under sentence were obliged to observe the interdict, nevertheless, a custom arose whereby people of an interdicted parish attended services in a neighboring parish. The Council of Cologne,[164] however, in the year 1279, put an end to this practice when it decreed that priests, before commencing services, should inquire as to whether any one present were from an interdicted place or parish, and if so, such person or persons must be expelled. The same Council decreed that priests neglecting their duty in this matter, incurred irregularity.[165] This regulation remained in force until changed by Pope Boniface VIII who permitted the revival of the former practice, save in the case of those who were responsible for the interdict.[166] It will be remembered that

160 C. 24, *de sent. excom.*, V, 11, in VI°.

161 Kober, *op. cit.*, XXI, 38.

162 Bellarmine, *Responsio ad Tract. Septem Theolo. Venet.*, Prop. VII.

163 Krehbiel, *op. cit.*, p. 46.

164 C. 18, Mansi, 24, 361.

165 *Ibidem.*

166 C. 24, *de sent. excom.*, V, 11, in VI°.

those who, by their misconduct, caused a local interdict to be imposed incurred a personal interdict.

During the latter part of the twelfth century and the first half of the thirteenth century, nearly all the chief countries of Western Europe were either interdicted or threatened with interdict. It is a fact worthy of note that Germany was threatened much less than the other countries of Europe; [167] the explanation probably lies in the fact that German prelates had little need to use the spiritual weapon of interdict, because many of them enjoyed much temporal authority. Interdicts were very frequent in Italy, France and Spain; they were more rare in England, Wales, Scotland and Denmark.[168]

Whether this censure, which has been so intimately connected with ecclesiastical and profane history, has ever been imposed in the New World, is a question concerning which much speculation has been made. Certainly there have been no cases of interdict comparable to the great interdicts inflicted on European countries during the twelfth and thirteenth centuries. That the New World has had interdicts on a smaller scale is evident from a statement made by the Council of Mexico in 1585: "Ne ministri ecclesiae, aut aliae quaecumque personae ob ignorantiam efficiant quod tempore interdicti, aut cessationis a divinis jure prohibitum est, haec synodus juxta contenta in capitulo, *Alma Mater*, declarat ab eis frequentes regulas observari." [169]

Of much interest is the case of an interdict in the diocese of Scranton in 1906. It happened that trouble arose in the Lithuanian parish of St. Joseph, with the result that the members of the parish authorized a committee to commence an action of litigation against the Rt. Rev. Michael Hoban, Bishop of Scranton. The purpose of this civil action was to secure a reconveyance of the parochial property from the Bishop to a committee of the members of the parish.[170] The case was carried to the Supreme Court of Pennsylvania,

[167] Krehbiel, *op. cit.*, p. 48.
[168] Krehbiel, *op. cit.*, p. 49.
[169] Hardouin, X, 1726.
[170] Zollmann, *American Civil Church Law*, p. 358.

and a decision was granted in favor of the parish to the effect that the members of the parish had the right to compel the Bishop to reconvey the parish property to a committee of members. The Bishop complied with the provisions of the Supreme Court, but he excommunicated the plaintiffs and placed the Church of Saint Joseph under an interdict "until the members of the congregation shall turn these faithless men out and place the church once more under the care of the Bishop of the Diocese of Scranton, according to the laws of the Catholic Church.[171] This interdict was not without its effect, for very soon the members of the parish set about to adjust matters with their Bishop.

In very recent times, the Holy See itself has found it necessary to inflict interdicts. Thus, in the year 1909, Bishop Boggiani of Adria was attacked by the people of the city, and Pope Pius X decreed that an interdict should be placed on the town for fifteen days "as a salutary punishment." This interdict was *general local* and *general personal* for the entire city and its suburbs. Consequently the following were forbidden: (1) the celebration of Mass and all other sacred functions; (2) the ringing of bells; (3) the public administration of the Sacraments; and (4) solemn funeral rites. The following were permitted: (1) the administration of Baptism to infants and Penance, Extreme Unction and Holy Viaticum to the dying; (2) the private celebration of Matrimony; and (3) the celebration of Mass once a week for renewing the Holy Eucharist.[172]

A similar interdict was imposed on the town of Galatina in the year 1913, with the same prohibitions and concessions.[173] This interdict was imposed on account of a sacrilegious attack on the venerable Archbishop of Otranto. In both cases, warning was given that violators of the interdict would sin gravely, and if the violators be priests, they would incur irregularity.

---

[171] Zollmann, *Ibidem.*

[172] *AAS,* I (1909), 765 ff.

[173] *AAS,* V (1913), 517.

PART II

THE EFFECTS OF THE INTERDICT

Necessary Preliminary Considerations

It seems necessary before commencing to comment upon the canons, to consider a few points which are so closely bound with the various effects of the interdict, that a clear knowledge of them is absolutely indispensable if one is to arrive at an understanding of the legislation of the canons. Accordingly, consideration must first be given to the provisions of Canon 2232, after which the distinction between a condemnatory sentence and a declaratory sentence must be discussed.

I.—The Provisions of Canon 2232

It is stated in Canon 2232, §1, that a *latae sententiae* penalty, whether it be medicinal or vindictive, binds the delinquent who is conscious of his delict, in both fora. It is further provided, however, that before a declaratory sentence is passed, the delinquent is excused from observing the penalty, as long as he is unable to observe it without infamy. Moreover, no one can demand the observance of such penalties in the external forum, unless the delinquent's delict is notorious.[1]

A penalty is *latae sententiae* when it is so connected with a given law that it is automatically and immediately incurred when the law is violated.[2] Inasmuch as the penalty is incurred automatically, the delinquent who is conscious of his delict must observe the penalty in both the internal and the external forum from the very moment of the com-

[1] Can. 2197, nn. 2,3.

[2] Can. 2217, §1, n. 2.

mission of the delict. This mode of punishment, unknown in civil law, is employed by the Church, because she considers certain laws so important, and the violation of them so serious, that she places a sanction on them without the apprehension of the delinquent or the intervention of a Superior. Therefore, the delinquent is obliged to observe a *latae sententiae* penalty in both fora, even if he is the only one who knows that the delict has been committed. From the very nature of the penalty itself, it is clear that the Superior need not act in order that the penalty be effective.

Although a *latae sententiae* penalty, *per se*, binds the delinquent to its observance in both fora, nevertheless, Canon 2232, §1, makes the further provision that the delinquent is excused from the obligation of observing the penalty whenever its observance would result in loss of his reputation, and, consequently, unless the delict itself be notorious, no one can force him to observe the penalty in the external forum. The Church in this matter wishes to safeguard the reputation even of her most disobedient children, consequently, as long as the delict is occult, there is no warrant even on the part of a Superior to make it public, which certainly would result if the delinquent were forced to observe a *latae sententiae* penalty resulting from an occult delict. Moreover, it would seem that the law would be demanding too much if it forced a delinquent practically to defame himself by undergoing public punishment for a delict which was committed privately, and which still remains occult.[3] In this connection, Vermeersch-Creusen remark: "Nemo enim seipsum prodere debet et contra omnem aequitatem cogatur quis ut contra se actus vindicativos exerceat." [4] Accordingly, Sole argues that the natural law urges the principle, "neminem teneri prodere seipsum." [5] In like manner, Ayrinhac [6] says that in this matter the principle is applied that no one should be punished

[3] Cappello, *De Censuris*, n. 74.

[4] *Epitome*, III, n. 426.

[5] *De Delictis et Poenis*, n. 126.

[6] *Penal Legislation*, p. 73.

unless his guilt is certain, and that in the public estimation, guilt is certain only when it has been declared as such in a judicial manner, or when the guilt itself is nortorious. But the question will naturally arise as to when a delict is to be considered notorious. To this question the Code itself answers that a delict is notorious when it is publicly known, or when it is committed under such circumstances that it is unable to be concealed by any artifice, or excused by any supplication of law.[7] From this definition of a notorious delict, it is evident that the delinquent must observe the penalty in both fora, since the delict is already publicly known and there is no longer any question of protecting the reputation of the delinquent.

In order to determine whether or not the penalty can be observed in the external forum without loss of reputation, attention must be given to the distinction between positive and negative penalties.[8] Thus, according to D'Annibale, "Poena...positiva ea dicitur que consistit in facto; idest quae sine facto aliquo nostro, vel alterius, subire non potest; ut puta publicatio bonorum, carcer, exilium, mulcta. Negativa ea est quae consistit in jure; id quae vel privat aliquo jure quaesito, velut officio, beneficio, jurisdictione, jure suffragii; vel acquirendi facit inhabilem; idest quae in odium patrati criminis nobis adimit capacitatem seu canonicam, seu civilem, seu naturalem faciendi, acquirendi, contrahendi." [9] With this distinction in mind, D'Annibale [10] further remarks that the delinquent regularly cannot observe the positive penalties without infamy; for the delinquent in placing an act necessary for the observance of the penalty, would be forced to betray himself. The same is to be said with regard to negative penalties which deprived the delinquent of an acquired right, e.g., a benefice or an office.[11] For, penalties of this kind consist in the privation of a right, and the observance of such a penalty necessitates some act or omission on the part of

[7] Can. 2197, n. 3.
[8] Sole, *op. cit.*, n. 127; Vermeersch-Creusen, *Epitome*, III, n. 426.
[9] *Summula Theologia Moralis*, I, n. 308.
[10] *Ibidem.*
[11] Sole, *op. cit.*, n. 127.

the delinquent or on the part of another. Thus, for example, the negative penalty of inhability to an already acquired office, cannot be observed without a public act of omission. Accordingly, when there is question of penalties of this kind, whether they be positive or negative, inasmuch as they deprive one of a right already acquired, the delinquent, regularly at least, is excused from observing them before a declaratory sentence has been passed.

But what is to be said of negative penalties which deprive one, not of a right already acquired, but which deprives him of his juridical capacity to acquire rights? An example would be the inability of acquiring benefices. It is the opinion of Sole [12] that these penalties can be observed without incurring the loss of the delinquent's reputation, and consequently, the delinquent must observe them even before the passing of a declaratory sentence.

It has been said that a *latae sententiae* penalty, whether medicinal or vindictive, *ipso facto* binds the delinquent conscious of it in both the internal and the external forum. Moreover, before a declaratory sentence is passed, the delinquent is excused from observing the penalty, as long as he cannot observe it without the loss of reputation, unless, of course, the delict be notorious. Consequently, with the exception of a notorious delict, no superior can force a delinquent to observe a *latae sententiae* penalty before a declaratory sentence has been passed. On the other hand, a superior can, if he considers it expedient, pronounce a declaratory sentence; indeed, he must do so if legitimately requested at the instance of an interested party, or if it be necessary for the sake of the public good.[13]

After the superior has pronounced the declaratory sentence, it is obvious that he can force the delinquent to observe the penalty already incurred. This legislation is wisely enacted, and accordingly, Sole remarks, "Et merito quidem, quia agitur de re gravissima in qua omni adhibita cautela procedendum est; ideoque antequam delinquens publice habeatur gravissimis poenis mulctatus, juridice de pa-

[12] *Op. cit.*, n. 128.

[13] Can. 2223, §4.

trato crimine constare debet." [14] The legitimate mode of procedure is the formal passing of a declaratory sentence by a competent judge.[15] In this connection, Lega writes: "Quo pacto evitatur dubietas ex parte *facti* et durities ex parte executionis poenae, quae a judice executioni demandatur, retroacto effectu poenae ad momentum criminis admissi." [16]

Thus, under the old law,[17] which provided that the goods of heretics were *ipso jure* confiscated, it was stipulated that the confiscation of these temporal goods was not effective until the Bishop of the place, or some other ecclesiastical person having authority in this matter, pronounced a sentence condemning the crime of heresy.

What has been said in the foregoing discussion concerning Canon 2232 must be constantly borne in mind in considering the effects of the interdict. This is important, because the provisions of this Canon are such that they have a practical bearing in the interpretation of all the canons soon to be considered. Finally, therefore, a delinquent who has incurred a *latae sententiae* penlaty is not obliged in law to observe it, unless the delict is notorious, or unless a declaratory sentence has been passed by a competent superior, or unless the delinquent can observe the penalty without incurring the odium of infamy.

II.—Meaning of Declaratory and Condemnatory Sentences

Throughout the discussion dealing with Canon 2232, it was frequently necessary to employ the term *sententia declaratoria.* It will likewise be necessary to make frequent use of the terms *sententia declartoria* and *sententia condemnatoria,* throughout the commentary of the canons to be considered presently. Consequently, a clear knowledge of the meaning of declaratory and condemnatory sentences is indispensable, if one is to arrive at an understanding as to the meaning of the legislation on interdicts.

---

[14] *Op. cit.,* n. 129.
[15] Can. 2210, §2; Can. 2225.
[16] *De Delictis et Poenis,* n. 87.
[17] C. 19, *de hereticis,* V, 11, in VI°.

A declaratory sentence is that which is pronounced only in the case of such penalties as are *latae sententiae;* a sentence of this kind does not impose a penalty, but merely proclaims that a certain one has committed a grave delict to which a *latae sententiae* penalty is connected, and that this penalty has consequently been incurred. Although, as has been said, a declaratory sentence does not inflict or impose a penalty, nevertheless, by it a delinquent is forced to observe a *latae sententiae* penalty which, heretofore, *servatis servandis,* he could not be forced to observe. Although a declaratory sentence does not impose a new penalty, but merely declares that a penalty has already been incurred, nevertheless it has the effect of putting into action a penalty which previously had been, what might be called, a mere potential penalty. It is to be admitted, however, that a declaratory sentence is never necessary, in order that a *latae sententiae* penalty be incurred, because a penalty of this kind is such that it automatically *(ipso facto)* binds a delinquent who is conscious of his delict in both fora. Such a sentence becomes necessary if the penalty is to have full force in the case where an interested party legitimately requests it, or if the common good demands it.[18] It will be remembered that before a declaratory sentence, a delinquent is not bound to observe a *latae sententiae* penalty, whenever such observance would result in the loss of reputation; hence, the only lawful manner of forcing him to observe the penalty is by the pronouncement of a declaratory sentence. Of course, if the delict in question be notorious, there is no longer any question of protecting the reputation of the delinquent; consequently, under such circumstances, he is bound to observe the penalty even before a declaratory sentence has been passed.

But when, and under what circumstances, should a superior pronounce a declaratory sentence? Aside from the two cases mentioned in Canon 2223, §4, in which he must do so, it is generally left to the prudent judgment of the superior to pronounce a declaratory sentence. With regard to the mode of procedure, in making the declaratory

[18] Can. 2223, §4.

sentence, it may be said that the superior may declare the penalty by a judicial sentence, or even extra-judicially, if the penalty were inflicted as a particular precept.[19] Furthermore, a declaratory sentence is of such a nature, that the penalty is effective not from the time that the declaratory sentence was issued, but from the very moment in which the delict was committed.[20]

Care must be taken not to confound the status of a delinquent whose delict is notorious and one upon whom a declaratory sentence has been pronounced. There is obviously a great difference between not being excused from observing a *latae sententiae* penalty and being subject to the grave canonical effects which a declaratory sentence entails.[21]

A condemnatory sentence is that whereby a penalty is imposed. Just as a dèclaratory sentence is employed only when there is question of *latae sententiae* penalties, so also, a condemnatory sentence is pronounced only in the case of *ferendae sententiae* penalties. A *ferendae sententiae* penalty is one which requires the action of a judge or other legitimate superior, in order that the penalty be incurred. In other words, there is no penalty until the sentence is passed by the judge.[22] According to Cerato, "Sententia condemnatoria item non nisi in judicio fertur, atque eam legitimus judex vel Superior competens atque agens ut judex, ad mormam canonum, delinquenti ob commissum et probatum delictum infligit seu applicat poenam vel censuram *ferendae sententiae,* quae violatae legi suae praecepto adnexa est, infligenda per judicem." [23] Thus, it is evident that a penalty so inflicted obtains only from the time it was inflicted by means of a condemnatory sentence; therefore, since, previous to the condemnatory sentence, the delinquent was not bound by a penalty, it is obvious that a condemnatory sentence really inflicts or imposes a penalty; such a penalty, therefore, is effective only from the moment in which the superior pronounces the condemnatory sentence.

---

[19] Can. 1933, §4; Cocchi, *Commentarium,* VIII, n. 46.

[20] Can. 2232, §2.

[21] Cappello, *De Censuris,* n. 76.

[22] Can. 2217, §1, n. 2.

[23] *Censurae Vigentes,* n. 8.

Prior to a condemnatory sentence, the penalty may have been *a jure,* i.e., when a determinate penalty is established by the law itself; after a condemnatory sentence, however, the penalty is both *a jure* and *ab homine,* but is considered *ab homine.*[24]

It is important, therefore, to distinguish carefully between these two types of sentences. Thus, to sum up: a declaratory sentence is pronounced only when there is question of a *latae sententiae* penalty; while a condemnatory sentence is pronounced only in the case of a *ferendae sententiae* penalty. Moreover, a declaratory sentence in no wise imposes or inflicts a penalty; it merely proclaims that a certain penalty has been incurred. A condemnatory sentence, on the other hand, really inflicts a penalty, because prior to the proclamation of the condemnatory sentence, the delinquent was not under a penalty. Furthermore, from the very nature of a declaratory sentence, it is evident that the penalty has its effect from the moment in which the delict was committed, because at that time the penalty was incurred; while the nature of a condemnatory sentence is such that it has its effect only from the time the sentence is pronounced. Finally, a declaratory sentence does not cause an *a jure* penalty to become *ab homine* also, although it is necessary that such a penalty be removed in the external forum by a competent superior.[25] A condemnatory sentence, on the other hand, causes an *a jure* penalty to become *ab homine.*[26]

The distinctions mentioned above must be carefully borne in mind when one is considering the canons which legislate on interdicts, because with regard to certain prohibitions, it makes a great difference whether or not a personally interdicted individual has had a condemnatory or a declaratory sentence pronounced against him. Moreover, mention of these sentences will frequently be necessary throughout the present discussion.

---

[24] Can. 2217, §1, n. 3.
[25] Cappello, *De Censuris,* n. 76.
[26] Can. 2217, §1, n. 3.

CHAPTER I

The Laying of an Interdict

Canon 2269.—§1. Generale interdictum tam locale in territorium diocesis, reipublicae, quam personale in populum diocesis, reipublicae, ferri tantum potest a Sede Apostolica vel de eius mandato; interdictum vero generale in paroeciam vel paroeciae populum, et particulare sive locale sive personale, etiam Episcopus ferre potest.

§2. Interdictum personale sequitur personas ubique; locale non urget extra locum interdictum, sed in loco interdicto omnes etiam exteri aut exempti, excluso speciali privilegio, illud servare debent.

I.—Authorities Competent to Impose Interdicts

A general local interdict which affects an entire diocese or country, or a general personal interdict which affects all the people of a diocese or country, can be imposed only by the Apostolic See, or by one specially delegated (by the Holy See) for this purpose. It is clear, therefore, that it is not within the power of a bishop to declare an interdict against his entire diocese, or against all the people of his diocese. Prior to the Code, there was much doubt as to the extent of a bishop's power in this regard,[1] but now the doubt is solved by Canon 2269, §1, which specifically states that this power is reserved to the Holy See. According to the canon under consideration, however, a bishop may impose a general local interdict on an entire parish, or a general personal interdict on all the people of a parish, and *a fortiori,* he can impose a particular interdict, whether it be local or personal, within the limits of his diocese.

---

[1] Vermeersch-Creusen, *Epitome,* III, n. 473.

It will be noticed that the term *Episcopus* is here employed, and, consequently, the Vicar General is not included. If it were the intention of the legislator to include the Vicar General, without doubt, the term *Ordinarius* would be employed.[2]

A new question may arise, namely, can all the bishops of a province or nation, united in a plenary council, inflict a general personal or a general local interdict on their province or country? From the wording of Canon 2269, §1, they cannot, because it is therein stated that this power belongs to the Holy See alone, and this expression is exclusive of every other inferior legislator or group of legislators. If, however, all the bishops of a nation were unanimous in their opinion that their respective country should be placed under the ban of a general local or personal interdict, it might easily happen that the Holy See would delegate the united body of bishops to impose the interdict. For, it is quite probable that the Holy See would decide that there must be a good reason for an interdict when all the bishops, or even a large majority of the bishops of a country, agree as to its necessity or expediency. And this seems all the more probable when it is remembered that no bishop, and especially no national Hierarchy, would be very anxious to have so severe a punishment imposed on their respective country unless there were grave and cogent reasons warranting such action. Furthermore, from the phrase, "vel de ejus mandato," it is evident that it is not always necessary for the Holy See to act directly in this matter; on the other hand, it is quite likely that the Episcopate of a given country would be delegated to inflict a general interdict upon their country if the Holy See deemed it necessary.

Regular Ordinaries, inasmuch as the jurisdiction which they enjoy is personal and not territorial, cannot impose local interdicts on parishes subject to them.[3] Even before the promulgation of the Code, Regular Ordinaries lacked

---

[2] Cerato, *Censurae Vigentes*, n. 91.

[3] Sole, *De Delictis et Poenis*, n. 235; Schmalzgrueber, Pars IV, tit. XXXIX, n. 341.

the right to impose local interdicts, although they seemed to have the right to impose personal interdicts on their subjects. According to the opinion of pre-Code authors,[4] Regular Ordinaries lost the right to inflict local interdicts through custom.

By virtue of the canon under consideration, a bishop may impose an interdict without the consent of the Chapter, although the old law required such consent.[5] A bishop may also inflict an interdict as a special precept *(per modum praecepti extra judicium)* provided, of course, that the delict is certain.[6]

It may be asked whether or not a bishop can interdict all the parishes in his diocese singly. From the basis of the canon under consideration, it seems that he cannot.[7] Such action on the part of the bishop may not be at variance with the letter of the law, but in no wise can it be reconciled with the spirit of the law. In fact, the interdicting of all the parishes of a diocese separately would have every appearance of a "fraus legis," because in effect, at least, it would amount to a general local interdict which Canon 2269, §1, forbids a bishop to impose.

II.—The Extent of the Personal and Local Interdict

Canon 2269, §2, considers the material extent of the personal and local interdict. Since in the wording of the canon no distinction is drawn between general and particular interdicts, both kinds are evidently included. Consequently, all the effects described in Canons 2274 and 2275 follow the persons upon whom the interdict has been imposed.[8]

The personal interdict follows the persons upon whom it is inflicted everywhere; the local interdict binds only within and not outside the place interdicted. Nevertheless,

---

[4] Schmalzgrueber, *loc. cit.;* Wernz, *Jus Decretalium,* VI, n. 220.

[5] C. 1, X, V, 31.

[6] Can. 1933, §4.

[7] Cerato, *op. cit.,* n. 91.

[8] Augustine, *Commentary,* VIII, 200.

within the interdicted territory all, including strangers and exempt persons, are obliged to observe it.

If a personal interdict is imposed on the people of a given place, the clergy are not obliged to observe it.[9] In like manner, if a personal interdict is imposed on the clergy, the laity are not included in the ban.[10] Furthermore, not even the Religious clergy are included in a sentence of interdict which is imposed on the *clergy*.[11] The reason for such an apparently strange provision of the law in excluding the Religious clergy, is that in penal matters the milder interpretation is always to be followed.[12] If, however, a Religious enjoys a secular benefice or office, he certainly would be included among the secular clergy.[13] An exception is also made in favor of the bishops. Thus, if a personal interdict is imposed upon the clergy, bishops are not included in the ban unless they are specially mentioned.[14] It is also the opinion of Cerato,[15] that clerics who have no office or benefice in the place of interdict are not bound by the censure. Likewise, if a general personal interdict is imposed upon the people, insane persons and those who have not yet arrived at the use of reason are not included.[16]

A local interdict binds only within the interdicted territory, but according to the wording of Canon 2269, §2, all persons within the place of interdict are included, even if they be strangers or exempt persons. The phrase "*excluso speciali privilegio*" implies that a special privilege is necessary to excuse anyone within the territory of a local interdict. Consequently, *exteri* or outsiders must observe the interdict as long as they remain within the territory under the ban. By the term *exempt* is here meant personal and

---

[9] Suarez, *De Censuris*, disp. 32; Cerato, *op. cit.*, n. 91.

[10] Cerato, *Ibidem*.

[11] Devoti, *op. cit.*, lib. III, tit. XIX, §1; Schmalzgrueber, Pars IV, tit. XXXIX, n. 338.

[12] Can. 2219, §1.

[13] Schmalzgrueber, Pars IV, tit. XXXIX, n. 339; Cipollini, *De Censuris Latae Sententiae*, n. 71.

[14] Canon 2227, §2; Reiffenstuel, lib. V, tit. XXXIX, n. 188.

[15] *Loc. cit.*

[16] Schmalzgrueber, Pars IV, tit. XXXIX, n. 335.

not local exemption.[17] The Code[18] grants exemption from the power of the local Ordinary to all Regulars and their novices, and even to women who are subject to Regular Superiors. The local interdict, however, is an exception to this exception; for Canon 615 states that exempt persons are free from the jurisdiction of the Ordinary of the place, except in cases expressed by the law itself. But Canon 2269, §2, expressly states that even exempt persons must observe a local interdict. It is also the opinion of Cipollini[19] that even he who imposes the local interdict, must observe it while staying in the interdicted territory. But, inasmuch as the local interdict has no force outside its territorial limits, persons of the interdicted district may enter a place not under the ban, and there attend or even celebrate services, unless, of course, such persons be under personal interdict.[20]

The *special privilege* mentioned in Canon 2269, §2, is one granted by the Holy See whereby further liturgical celebrations in the churches within the interdicted territory are permitted. Thus, in virtue of a privilege granted the Friars Minor by Pope Clement VIII, they may *solemnly* celebrate certain feasts of the Order.[21]

---

[17] Augustine, *op. cit.*, VIII, 200.

[18] Can. 615.

[19] *Op. cit.*, n. 74.

[20] Cipollini, *loc. cit.*

[21] "Sacrae Seraphici beati Francisci religionis in Sanctam Romanam Ecclesiam merita poscunt, ut privilegia et indulta illi per Sedem Apostolicam concessa non modo conserventur sed etiam amplientur. Cum itaque sicut accepimus diversorum Romanorum Pontificum concessionibus religioni praefatae indultum sit, ut temporibus interdicti, quacumque etiam apostolica auctoritate appositi, festa Sanctorum ejusdem Ordinis S. Francisci nimirum S. Bonaventurae, Sancti Antonii de Padua, Sancti Ludovici, S. Bernardini, Sanctae Clarae, Sanctae Elizabeth ac Sanctorum Martyrum solemni ritu celebrare, perinde ac si interdictum hujusmodi minime appositum esset, libere possint: festa vero S. Didaci et Portiunculae in praedicto indulto minime comprehendantur. Nos religionem praedictam amplioribus favoribus et gratiis prosequi volentes, ac indultorum hujusmodi et literarum apostolicarum desuper expeditarum tenores, praesentibus pro expressis habentes, supplicationibus dictae religionis per dilectum filium nostrum Hieronymum presbyterum cardinalem Matthaeum nobis super hoc humiliter porrectis inclinati, religioni praedictae universae ac cuicumque ipsius ordinis sive familiae et conventui, ut in eorum ecclesiis

The Constitution states that these feasts may be celebrated *solemni ritu,* by which it is clear that the celebration may be marked with all the splendor with which these feasts would be celebrated if there were no interdict at all. Concerning this privilege Lyszczarczyk [22] states that the feasts mentioned may be celebrated *januis apertis,* which would indicate that the faithful in general may be admitted to the services.

Whether or not this privilege can be invoked by other Orders by way of communication of privileges is a much controverted point.[23]

festa etiam praedicti S. Didaci et Portiunculae temporibus interdicti solemniter prout alia festa praedicta, ac juxta indultorum illi concessorum seriem et tenorem celebrare libere et licite possint, auctoritate apostolica tenore praesentium concedimus et indulgemus ac indulta praedicta ad praedictas S. Didaci et Portiunculae festivitates extendimus et ampliamus."—Const. "*Sacrae Seraphici,*" Oct. 17, 1595, apud Wadding, *Annales Minorum,* XXIII, p. 452.

[22] *Compendium Privilegiorum Regularium,* p. 45.

[23] Piat, *Praelectiones Juris Regularis,* Vol. II, p. 79, q. 3, n. 4.

CHAPTER II

MODIFYING CONSEQUENCES OF THE LOCAL INTERDICT

Canon 2270.—§1. Interdictum locale sive generale sive particulare non vetat morientibus Sacramenta et Sacramentalia, servatis servandis, ministrare, sed prohibet in loco quodlibet divinum officium vel sacrum ritum, salvis exceptionibus de quibus in §2 hujus canonis et in can. 2271, 2272.

§2. In die Nativitatis Domini, Paschatis, Pentecostes, sanctissimi Corporis Christi et Beatae Mariae Virginis in caelum assumptae interdictum locale suspenditur, et prohibetur tantum collatio ordinum et sollemnis nuptiarum benedictio.

Canon 2270, §1, treats of the consequences of the local interdict, whether the interdict be general or particular. Thus, according to the canon under consideration, no divine office or sacred rite is permitted in any place over which a general or particular local interdict has been imposed. This is the general statement of the law; there are, however, many concessions which shall be considered presently.

It seems fitting and proper, before considering the exceptions from the law, to endeavor to arrive at the meaning of the term *divine offices* (officia divina). By this term is understood all the various functions proper to the power of Orders, which are ordained by the institution of Christ or the Church for divine worship, and can be performed only by clerics.[1] Now, among the divine offices are, in the first place, the Holy Sacrifice of the Mass, the recitation of the Canonical Hours in choir, public processions, Benediction of the Most Blessed Sacrament, the blessing of ashes, water, candles and palms; moreover, all consecrations are included, such as the consecration of altars and chalices. In other

[1] Can. 2256, n. 1.

words, all ceremonies instituted by Christ or His Church for divine worship, and which can be performed only by those enjoying the power of Orders.[2] Hence many other popular devotions such as the public recitation of the Rosary, the Stations of the Cross are not included among the divine offices in the technical use of the term.[3]

I.—Concessions Granted According to Canon 2270

As has already been said, there are many exceptions mitigating to a very great extent the severity of the local interdict. Hence Canon 2270, §1, makes a broad concession in favor of the dying during the time of a local interdict. It will be remembered that this canon makes no distinction between general and particular interdicts. Therefore, neither a general nor a particular local interdict forbids the administration of the Sacraments and Sacramentals to the dying. Among the Sacraments of the dying the Sacrament of Extreme Unction is also included.[4] Before the Code there was an opinion that Extreme Unction, inasmuch as it was not absolutely necessary for salvation, was not permitted during the time of a local interdict.[5] It was the opinion of authors that if the dying person was already destitute of his senses, and therefore unable to make his confession, Extreme Unction could be administered.[6] With regard to this concession in favor of the dying, Canon 2270, §1, employs the expression "servatis servandis" which according to the Code[7] means that Holy Viaticum must be carried *privately* to the dying during a general local interdict.

Canon 2270, §2, states that on the great festivals of Christmas, Easter, Pentecost, Corpus Christi and the

---

[2] Schmalzgrueber, Pars IV, tit. XXXIX, n. 360 ff; Cappello, *De Censuris*, n. 149.

[3] Augustine, *Commentary*, VIII, 177.

[4] Reiffenstuel, lib. V, tit. XXXIX, n. 203; Augustine, *op. cit.*, VIII, p. 204.

[5] Lega, *De Delictis et Poenis*, n. 179.

[6] Lehmkuhl, *Th. Mor.* II, 908; D'Annibale, *op. cit.*, III, n. 374, nota 37; Bouuaert-Simenon, *Manuale Juris Canonici*, n. 1289.

[7] Can. 2271, n. 2.

Assumption of the Blessed Virgin Mary, a local interdict is suspended. Consequently, on those feasts, solemn services may be held according to the full liturgy of the Church. There are, however, two exceptions to this general concession; the conferring of Orders and the solemn nuptial blessings are forbidden on the above-named feasts.

It will be noticed that the Canon under consideration uses the phrase "in die," which signifies that the privilege extends only throughout the feast-day itself and not throughout the octave. It is true that the extension of this privilege throughout the octave of the feast of Corpus Christi was granted by Pope Eugene IV, May 26, 1433, in his decree, "Excellentissimum," [8] but since the Code makes no mention of it, this extension of the privilege must be considered as abrogated. It is the opinion of Augustine,[9] however, that when the celebration of Corpus Christi is transferred to the following Sunday, the local interdict is then suspended. It is the opinion of Vermeersch-Creusen [10] that the privilege granted to Spain by Pope Leo X, whereby the feast of the Immaculate Conception of the Blessed Virgin was numbered among the privileged feasts, still obtains.

II.—Concessions During the Time of a General Local Interdict

Canon 2271.—Si interdictum fuerit locale generale et interdicti decreto aliud non caveatur expresse:

n. 1. Permittitur clericis, dummodo non sint ipsi personaliter interdicti, omnia divina officia et sacros ritus in quacumque ecclesia aut oratorio privatim obire, ianuis clausis, voce submissa et campanis non pulsatis;

n. 2. In ecclesia vero cathedrali, ecclesiis paroecialibus vel in ecclesia quae unica sit in oppido, in iisque solis, permittuntur unius Missae celebratio, asservatio sanctissimi Sacramenti, administratio baptismatis, Eucharistiae, poenitentiae, assistentia matrimoniis, exclusa benedictione nuptiali, mortuorum exequiae,

[8] *Fontes*, n. 48.

[9] *Commentary*, VIII, 204.

[10] *Epitome*, III, n. 476.

vetita tamen quavis sollemnitate, benedictio aquae baptismalis et sacrorum oleorum, praedicatio verbi Dei. In his tamen sacris functionibus prohibetur cantus et pompa in sacrae supellectili et sonitus campanarum, organorum, aliorumve instrumentorum musicalium; sacrum autem Viaticum ad infirmos privatim deferatur.

Canon 2271 states the modifications which obtain during the time of a general local interdict. In the first place, however, it may be stated that the concessions granted by this Canon are not absolute; in other words, it must be remembered that these concessions obtain, *unless the decree of interdict expressly contains something to the contrary.* It must also be kept in mind that the effects of the interdict are divisible, and this is one of the respects in which the interdict differs from excommunication.[11]

The privilege granted in §1 of Canon 2271 concerns the clergy only. Accordingly, clerics, unless they be personally interdicted, may privately perform all the divine offices and sacred ceremonies in any church or oratory during the time of a general local interdict, provided such offices and ceremonies are conducted in a low tone of voice and without the ringing of bells. It will be noticed that the use of this concession depends entirely on the status of the cleric seeking to avail himself of it. In other words, a cleric may not make use of this privilege if he is bound by a personal interdict; for anyone bound by a personal interdict is forbidden to celebrate divine offices, and, with the exception of the preaching of the word of God, such a person is even forbidden to assist at them.[12]

A church is a sacred edifice dedicated to divine worship especially with the view of enabling all the faithful to practice public worship therein.[13] An oratory, on the other hand, is a place destined for divine worship, not however for the purpose that all the faithful may publicly practice worship therein.[14] There are three kinds of oratories:

[11] Can. 2257.
[12] Can. 2275, n. 1, cfr. Can. 2338, §4.
[13] Can. 1161.
[14] Can. 1188, §1.

public, semi-public and private oratories. A public oratory is one which is erected for the convenience of a group or even of private individuals, in such a manner, however, that all the faithful are permitted to enter it, at least during the celebration of divine offices.[15] A semi-public oratory is one which is erected for the convenience of a community or group of the faithful, and not for the use of all the faithful.[16] A private oratory is one which is erected in a private edifice for the use of a family or private individual.[17] Accordingly, the privilege stated in Canon 2271, n. 1, may be exercised in any church or in any oratory, provided, of course, that the other requirements are fulfilled. Among these stipulations and requirements are the following: the Canon uses the term *privatim,* which signifies that the services must be conducted in private, i.e., without solemnity; the term *ianuis clausis* signifies that the faithful must not be admitted.[18] It was the opinion of Reiffenstuel,[19] however, that the faithful who were not personally interdicted could assist at these services, but the term *ianuis clausis* certainly contains an implicit prohibition against the attendance at the divine services permitted by virtue of Canon 2271, n. 1. According to the present discipline, however, the question is of minor importance, since at least in one church in every town or city the faithful may assist at the Sacrifice of the Mass and receive the Sacraments.[20] Augustine,[21] is of the opinion that if a priest has no server to serve his Mass, a layman may be admitted for this purpose.

It is further required that the divine services must be carried on *voce submissa,* i.e., in a low tone of voice, so that those outside can in no wise follow the prayers recited during the course of the services.[22] It may also be rightly in-

---

15 Can. 1188, §2, n. 1.
16 Can. 1188, §2, n. 2.
17 Can. 1188, §2, n. 3.
18 Suarez, *De Censuris,* disp. XXXIV, sect. 1, n. 21.
19 Lib. V, tit. XXXIX, n. 310 ff.
20 Vermeersch-Creusen, *Epitome,* III, n. 476.
21 *Commentary,* VIII, 205.
22 Suarez, *loc. cit.,* n. 12.

ferred that the words, *voce submissa,* exclude chanting of any kind. It is further provided that the services must be conducted without the ringing of bells. It seems, however, that this prohibition does not forbid the ringing of the bell for the "Angelus" nor for the preaching of the word of God.[23] According to Schmalzgrueber,[24] the prohibition against the ringing of bells in connection with these services has reference to the ringing of the bell at the "Sanctus" of the Mass and at the elevation of the Sacred Host and the Chalice. He maintains that bells may be rung for the "Angelus," also for calling the faithful for preaching the word of God. The concession just considered has reference to the clergy only; now consideration will be given to a further concession which the faithful also may enjoy.

Canon 2271, n. 2, treats of a concession in favor of all the faithful. Herein a privilege is granted whereby cathedral churches, parish churches, and any church which is the only one in town enjoy the exemptions about to be enumerated. Accordingly, in all such churches as have just been mentioned, and in those only, one Mass may be celebrated daily; the reservation of the Blessed Sacrament is permitted; priests may administer the Sacrament of Baptism together with all its ceremonies; the Sacraments of Penance and Holy Eucharist may be administered; priests may assist at marriages, but may not give the nuptial blessing; the burial of the dead is permitted, but without any solemnity; the blessing of baptismal water and holy oils is permitted, and, finally, the preaching of the Word of God. In these sacred functions, however, chanting and pomp in the sacred furnishings are forbidden; the same is true of the ringing of the bells and the playing of organs and other musical instruments; finally, Holy Viaticum must be carried privately to the dying.

It will be noticed that §2 of Canon 2271 employs the phrase "in ecclesia vero cathedrali, ecclesiis paroecialibus vel in ecclesia quae unica sit in oppido." From this phrase

---

[23] C. 11, X, *de poenit.*, V, 38; Suarez, *loc. cit.*, n. 16 ff.

[24] Pars IV, tit. XXXIX, n. 366.

it is evident that there must be churches which are neither cathedral churches nor parochial churches. It so happens that certain confraternities can possess their own churches, and exercise functions in them, *servatis servandis,* independently of the local pastor, provided that such services do not work harm to the parish in which such a church may exist.[25] It might easily happen that such a church may be established by a given confraternity in a small town or village in which no parish has as yet been established. Consequently, if a diocese, for example, were placed under a general local interdict, and if in that diocese there be a town which has no parish church, but which has situated in it the church of a confraternity, such a church may enjoy all the privileges narrated in Canon 2271, n. 2, as long as it is an *ecclesia quae unica sit in oppido.* It is evident, of course, that such churches do not enjoy the privileges of Canon 2271, n. 2, if even one parish church exists in the same town with them.

Since no restriction is made by the Code as to the number of parish churches which may enjoy these privileges, any and every parish church may share them, even though there may be several parish churches in a city or town. Moreover, it seems that public oratories, inasmuch as they fall under the same regulations as churches,[26] may also benefit by the concessions now being considered, if there be no other church in the town or city. Consequently, if the faithful of a given district have been wont to attend Mass and other functions in a public oratory, because as yet no parish has been established in their district, certainly such a public oratory should be considered as enjoying the concessions stated in Canon 2271, n. 2. This seems all the more probable when it is remembered that there is here a question of a privilege from a penal measure, and, therefore, the more favorable interpretation is to be followed.[27]

---

[25] Can. 710, §1.
[26] Can. 1191, §1.
[27] Can. 2219, §1.

From the wording of the Canon, it seems that the privileges therein stated cannot be extended to semi-public or private oratories, because neither of these types of oratories is governed by the same regulations as churches,[28] nor have the faithful a real right to attend services in them.[29] The Code is somewhat stricter than the old law in this regard.[30] Thus, it was the opinion of authors[31] that even private oratories shared the privileges granted during the time of a general local interdict. According to the present discipline of the law, as stated in Canon 2271, n. 2, it is difficult to see how this position can now be held, because the canon, after enumerating the churches which enjoy these privileges, employs the phrase, "in iisque solis," which certainly excludes semi-public and private oratories. Furthermore, as Augustine[31] points out, the favor granted in this canon is intended for the benefit of all the faithful and not for a private group or privileged class.

Among the privileges mentioned in Canon 2271, n. 2, is, first of all, the permission to celebrate one Mass in all churches according to the provisions mentioned in this canon. Although the Code does not state that this one Mass may be celebrated *daily*, it is the opinion of authors[32] that one Mass may be celebrated daily in all the churches sharing the privilege.

According to the old law,[33] the privilege was granted of celebrating Mass only once a week during the time of a general local interdict, but even in the time of Boniface VIII, this privilege was extended so as to permit the daily celebration of Mass in all the churches sharing the privilege.[34]

From the provision which forbids chanting and the playing of organs and other musical instruments, it is evident

---

[28] Can. 1191, §1.

[29] Can. 1188, §2, nn. 2, 3.

[30] C. 24, V, 11, in VI°.

[31] Suarez, *loc. cit.*, n. 5; Hilarius a Sexten, *Tract. de Cen.* p. 88.

[31] *Commentary*, VIII, 206.

[32] Augustine, *Commentary*, VIII, 206; Vermeersch-Creusen, *Epitome*, III, n. 476.

[33] C. 57, X, *de sent. excom.* V, 39.

[34] C. 24, *de sent. excom.* V, 11, in VI°.

that the daily Mass permitted according to Canon 2271, n. 2, must be a *low* Mass, because any attempt to celebrate a *Missa Cantata* or a Solemn Mass without chanting would be quite inconceivable. Furthermore, it would seem that the restriction forbidding any display of pomp or ceremony certainly excludes the possibility of celebrating a *Missa Cantata* or a Solemn Mass.

It will be remembered that with regard to funeral services, the canon states that all solemnity must be avoided. The Code [35] defines ecclesiastical burial as the transferring of the corpse to the church, the celebration of obsequies over it, and depositing it in a place legitimately assigned for the burial of the faithful departed. It would seem that Mass may be celebrated in connection with the burial of the faithful, but any additional solemnities must be excluded.

---

[35] Can. 1204.

CHAPTER III

EFFECTS OF THE PARTICULAR LOCAL INTERDICT

Canon 2272.—§1. In interdicto locali particulari, si interdictum fuerit altare vel sacellum alicuius ecclesiae, nullum sacrum officium seu sacer ritus in eisdem celebretur.

§2. Si interdictum fuerit coemeterium, fidelium quidem cadavera sepeliri ibidem possunt, sed sine ullo ecclesiastico ritu.

§3. Si latum fuerit in certam ecclesiam vel oratorium:

n. 2. Si ecclesia fuerit capitularis nec interdictum sit Capitulum, valet praescriptum can. 2271, n. 1, nisi interdicti decretum praecipiat Missam conventualem celebrari et horas canonicas recitari in alia ecclesia aut oratorio;

n. 2. Si fuerit paroecialis, servetur praescriptum cit. can. 2271, n. 2, nisi interdicti decretum aliam ecclesiam pro interdicti tempore eidem substituat.

I.—Interdicted Altars and Chapels

Canon 2272, §1, describes the effects of the particular local interdict. Therein it is stated that if an altar or chapel of any church is interdicted, no sacred office or sacred rite may be celebrated there. The wording of the canon is so absolute and exclusive that it seems to admit of no exception, for it is stated, "nullum sacrum officium seu sacer ritus in eisdem celebretur." It seems, therefore, that even such devotions as are not strictly liturgical, which do not come under the heading of *divine offices,* are forbidden by the provision of Canon 2272, §1.[1]

Although it is true that §1 of Canon 2272 is quite universal in its prohibition against the celebration of sacred offices and sacred rites, nevertheless it must be admitted that the exception stated in Canon 2270, §2 obtains also for the

[1] Augustine, *Commentary,* VIII, 207.

particular local interdict. Hence, if an altar or chapel be under a particular local interdict, this interdict is suspended on the feasts of Christmas, Easter, Pentecost, Corpus Christi, and the Assumption of the Blessed Virgin Mary. The reason for this interpretation is that Canon 2270, §2, states that on the feasts just mentioned, a local interdict is suspended; it simply states that a *local interdict* is suspended, making no distinction between general and particular local interdicts. Consequently, when the legislator makes no distinction, we need not distinguish.

II.—Interdicted Cemeteries

A cemetery intended for the sepulture of the faithful must be blessed by a solemn or simple benediction according to the rites contained in the approved liturgical books.[2] Canon 2272, §2, states the prohibitions which arise when a cemetery is interdicted. It is therein stated that during the time of an interdict against a cemetery, the bodies of the faithful may be interred there but without any ecclesiastical rite. It would seem to be no violation of the law, however, to supplement the burial with ecclesiastical rites at the grave after the interdict has been lifted.[3]

When a cemetery is under a particular local interdict, the exception mentioned in Canon 2270, §2, obtains. For, when a cemetery is placed under interdict, such an interdict is always local, and Canon 2270, §2, simply states that a local interdict, without distinguishing between general and particular interdicts, is suspended on the feasts of Christmas, Easter, Pentecost, Corpus Christi and the Assumption of the Blessed Virgin Mary. Consequently, the interdict against a cemetery, being local, is certainly suspended on those feasts, because the canon makes no distinction, and therefore there is no need for further distinction on our part. Concerning this matter, Sole writes: "Eapropter si interdictum fuerit coemeterium, in die Nativitatis Domini, Paschatis, etc., fidelium cadavera sepeliri ibidem possunt

---

[2] Can. 1205.

[3] Augustine, *Commentary*, VIII, 207.

cum ecclesiastico ritu, perinde ac nullum adesset interdictum."[4]

III.—Interdicts against Capitular and Parochial Churches

Canon 2272, §3, speaks of the effects of a particular local interdict when there is question of a designated church or oratory. Thus, if a designated church is placed under a particular local interdict, and it happens to be a capitular church, the canons of the chapter may avail themselves of the favor granted to the clergy in Canon 2271, n. 1. Of course, they cannot benefit by this favor if they themselves be under personal interdict; nor can this privilege be used if the decree of interdict states that Mass must be celebrated and the canonical hours recited in some other church or oratory. If the decree of interdict carried such a stipulation, it would be quite evident that no divine offices could be celebrated in the interdicted church of the chapter.

If the interdicted church be a parish church, the provision of Canon 2271, n. 1, has application. Consequently, the clergy, provided they are not themselves under personal interdict, may celebrate all the divine offices and sacred rites in a low tone of voice, without the ringing of bells, and privately, i.e., the faithful must be excluded.

---

[4] *De Delictis et Poenis.*, n. 241.

CHAPTER IV

The Extent of Local Interdicts

Canon 2273.—Interdicta civitate, interdicta quoque manen; loca accessoria etiam exempta et ipsa ecclesia cathedralist interdicta ecclesia, interdicta sunt sacella contigua, non vero coemeterium; interdicto sacello, non est interdicta integra ecclesia nec, interdicto coemeterio, interdicta est ecclesia ipsi contigua, sed interdicta sunt omnia oratoria in coemeterio erecta.

Canon 2273 treats of the material extent of a local interdict. Thus, if an interdict is imposed upon a city, the accessory places are also included in the interdicted territory. This is true even of exempt places and of the cathedral church itself. Accessory places are included when the principal city is placed under a local interdict, because "accessorium sequitur principale." [1] It seems that suburbs must be considered as *loca accessoria,* unless they are politically distinct from the city: "in toto partem non est dubium contineri." [2] Concerning the question of suburbs, many real difficulties may arise. Thus, to state that a given community is, or is not, a suburb of the neighboring city, is not always an easy matter. Schmalzgrueber [3] lays down a rule which has certain value in deciding individual cases: he states that a neighboring territory may be considered a suburb when it is so close to the principal city that the people of the so-called suburb are able, without grave difficulty, to attend divine services in the city. In determining what is meant by the term "loca accessoria," one can do no better than examine the Decretals of Pope

[1] *Reg.* 42, R. J., in VI°.

[2] *Reg.* 80, R. J., in VI°.

[3] Pars IV, tit. XXXIX, n. 326.

Boniface VIII. Therein he states that *loca accessoria* are "suburbia et continentia aedificia." [4] The great Pontiff explained that suburbs were affected by an interdict imposed upon the neighboring city, because the sentence of interdict would be ignored if divine offices could be lawfully celebrated in the suburbs.[5] Concerning the point in question, Cappello writes: "Interdicta civitate, manent interdicta loca accessoria, nempe aedificia propinqua, quae non distent ab urbe, ut aiunt, ultra mille passus circiter; si autem ulterius absint vel, etsi infra sita, difficilem accessum habeant, censentur non comprehendi. Ita antiquitus, quia civitas intelligebatur 'inter muros,' et loca continentia, quae non ultra milliare distarent. Hodie, muris fere ubique deiectis, res ex aliis criteriis iuridicis dimentienda est." [6]

There seems to be a difficulty concerning suburbs when they are under the jurisdiction of another Bishop. Concerning this matter, Sole [6a] proposes an opinion which is difficult to support. Thus, he states that it makes no difference whether suburbs or *loca accessoria* belong to the diocese of another Bishop or not. Therefore, he makes the conclusion: "...si Episcopus ferat interdictum generale in aliquam paroeciam (Can. 2269, §1), auctoritate iuris communis attingere valet etiam alterius diocesis loca, et eiús est denunciare nomiatim quaenam sint hujusmodi loca." [7] It certainly does not seem very likely that this provision concerning suburbs can be extended so as to cover two different territories with two different Ordinaries. Consequently, if a city which is a political unit is interdicted, and if such a city extends into the territory of another diocese, the territory which extends into the adjoining diocese should in no manner be affected by the interdict. For example, New York City and Brooklyn form one political territory; if, however, an interdict is imposed on New York City, Brooklyn should not be included in the interdict, for the simple reason that Brooklyn is a distinctly different diocese

[4] C. 17, *de sent. excom.* V. 11, in VI°.
[5] *Ibidem.*
[6] *De Censuris,* n. 470.
[6a] *De Delictis et Poenis,* n. 242.
[7] *Ibidem.*

from the City of New York. Cappello likewise holds the opinion that an interdict cannot be extended to such suburbs as are situated in the territory of another diocese. Hence he writes: "Controvertitur, utrum comprehendantur etiam loca aliis Episcopis forte subjecta, ita ut extra terminos diocesis interdictum generale vim suam obtineat. In iure antiquo haec loca censebantur comprehendi. Iure hodie vigente, verius negandum. Quare loca *exempta* ea censentur, quae intra fines diocesis exsistunt, licet Episcopi iurisdictioni non subsint, v. g., monasterium."[8] Of course, it is to be admitted that the Holy See could very easily impose an interdict which would include territory in two different dioceses, but such a case does not, strictly speaking, come within the scope of the present discussion.[9]

If an individual church is placed under a local interdict, the contiguous chapels are also included under the ban. An exception, however, is made in favor of the cemetery adjoining the church. Consequently, when a given church is placed under interdict, unless the sentence plainly states that the cemetery is included, there can be no doubt that the cemetery is free from interdict. The contiguous chapels of a church are included when the church itself is interdicted, because *accessorium sequitur principale.*[10] The cemetery, on the other hand, is considered as something distinct from the church, as is evident from the Code itself in Canon 1172, §2, wherein it is stated that whenever a church is violated, the cemetery, although contiguous, is not considered violated, and vice versa.

It is stated in Canon 2273 that even the cathedral church is included in the interdict when the city is placed under the ban. It seems, however, that the cathedral church is not included if the sentence of interdict is directed against *all the churches* of the city, and not the city itself.[11] The

---

[8] *De Censuris*, n. 470.

[9] Augustine, *Commentary*, VIII, 208.

[10] *Reg.* 42, R. J., in VI°.

[11] Cappello, *op. cit.*, n. 470.

reason for the exemption of the cathedral church is its pre-eminence, dignity and honor.[12]

If a certain chapel of a church is interdicted, the entire church is not interdicted; consequently it must be borne in mind that *accessorium sequitur principale,* but not vice versa. In like manner, if a cemetery is placed under interdict, the adjoining church is not included; this is evident from the distinction made in Canon 1172, §2. It is to be remembered, however, that all the oratories in a cemetery are affected by an interdict which is imposed upon the cemetery in which they are erected. This provision naturally follows from the principle, "in toto partem non est dubium contineri." [13] Consequently, it is clear that all the chapels or oratories erected in a given cemetery, are under the ban when the cemetery, of which they really form a part, is placed under interdict.

---

[12] Schmalzgrueber, Pars IV, tit. XXXIX, n. 327; Sole, *De Delictis et Poenis,* n. 242.

[13] *Reg.* 80, R. J., in VI°.

CHAPTER V

THE EFFECTS OF A PERSONAL INTERDICT

Canon 2274.—§1. Si communitas seu collegium delictum perpetraverit, interdictum ferri potest vel in singulas personas delinquentes, vel in communitatem uti talem, vel in personas delinquentes et in communitatem.

§2. Si primum, servetur praescriptum can. 2275.

§3. Si alterum, communitas seu collegium nequit ius ullum spirituale exercere quod ei competat.

§4. Si tertium, effectus cumulantur.

Canon 2275.—Personaliter interdicti:

n. 1. Nequeunt divina officia celebrare eisve, excepta praedicatione verbi Dei, assistere; passive assistentes non est necesse ut expellantur; sed ab assistentia activa, quae aliquam secumferat participationem in divinis officiis celebrandis, repellantur interdicti post latam sententiam condemnatoriam vel declaratoriam, aut alioquin notorie interdicti;

n. 2. Prohibentur Sacramenta et Sacramentalia ministrare, conficere et recipere, ad normam can. 2260, §1, 2261;

n. 3. Praecripto can. 2265 etiam ipsi adstringuntur;

n. 4. Carent sepultura ecclesiastica ad normam can. 1240, §1, n. 2.

Canon 2274 considers the effects of the personal interdict with due regard as to whether the interdict is particular or general. It will be remembered that a personal interdict may be imposed upon a collective body as such or upon the individual members of the body.

From the wording of Canon 2274, it seems that a distinction must be drawn between the terms "communitas" and "collegium." Thus, according to Augustine,[1] a *com-*

[1] *Commentary*, VIII, 211.

munitas is a society not closely organized, as, for instance, a parish, diocese or province. A *collegium,* on the other hand, is a more solidly organized society, such as, for example, cathedral and monastic chapters, provided, of course, they have their own constitutions and enjoy autonomy.

It is a recognized fact that such bodies as have just been described, inasmuch as they act collectively, as it were, with one will, are capable of committing a crime collectively, and therefore can be punished collectively. Hence if a university, college, chapter, or any other similar moral bodies appeal to a Universal Council against the mandates, laws or decrees of the reigning Pontiff, such a body incurs a personal interdict *speciali modo* reserved to the Holy See.[2] Likewise, a person who causes a local interdict to be imposed, or who causes a general personal interdict to be imposed upon a community or college, automatically (ipso facto) incurs a particular personal interdict.[3]

Canon 2274, §1, states that if a community or college commits a delict, there are three possible ways of inflicting a penalty on such a community or college. First of all, each individual member may be punished separately by means of a special personal interdict; secondly, a general personal interdict may be inflicted upon the community as such; and, finally, the penalty may be inflicted both on the individual members and upon the community as such.

If each individual member of a community is interdicted separately then the provisions of Canon 2275 must be applied; for in this case a particular personal interdict is imposed on each individual member of the moral body.

If the personal interdict is imposed upon the community as such, no moral right which belongs to the community as such can be exercised, although each individual member may continue to exercise the rights which he enjoys as an individual member.[4] Among the rights which a community may not exercise after a general personal interdict is declared against them, are: the right of election,[5] nomination

[2] Can. 2332.
[3] Can. 2338, §4.
[4] Crnica, *op. cit.*, p. 169; Sole, *De Delictis et Poenis*, n. 244.
[5] Can. 161.

and presentation.[6] Therefore, a chapter, if placed under a personal interdict, is deprived of its right to elect a Vicar Capitular[7] during the vacancy of the Episcopal See, or to confer benefices.[8] With regard to diocesan Consultors,[9] who, according to Augustine,[10] form a species of collegiate body, it seems that they would lose their right to elect an Administrator (during the vacancy of the See), if a personal interdict were imposed upon them.

According to Canon 2274, §4, the effects of a personal interdict may be doubled. Thus, if a community or college commits a delict, a personal interdict may be imposed on the community or college as such, and, at the same time, upon each member of the collegiate body. In other words, in this case there would be what might be called as a *double* interdict; i.e., each individual of the corporate body is affected by the interdict which is imposed upon the body as such, and, at the same time, he must observe the regulations for the personally interdicted according to the provisions of Canon 2275. In order that an interdict may have this double effect, however, it is necessary that it be plainly stated in the decree or sentence of interdict; otherwise there is room for the presumption that the sentence effects the body as such, and not each individual member as such.[11] This manner of doubling the effects of the personal interdict, i.e., by imposing it on the community as such, and, at the same time, on each individual member of the community, is a new mode of penal procedure in Canon Law with regard to the interdict.[12]

I.—Assistance at Divine Offices

Canon 2275 considers the effects of the particular personal interdict. Authors[13] consider this type of interdict

---

[6] Augustine, *Commentary*, VIII, 211; cfr. Can. 2265, §1, n. 1.
[7] Can. 432.
[8] Sole, *De Delictis et Poenis*, n. 244.
[9] Can. 427.
[10] *Commentary*, VIII, 212.
[11] Augustine, *Commentary*, VIII, 212.
[12] Crnica, *op. cit.*, p. 169.
[13] Sole, *op. cit.*, n. 245; Lega, *De Delictis et Poenis*, n. 170.

as a perfect type of censure, because it is incurred only on account of one's own guilt. Furthermore, when a particular personal interdict is imposed, an element of contumacy is always present.[14] Furthermore, a much graver delict is required to incur a personal interdict than to incur suspension, because the personal interdict bears a closer resemblance to excommunication, the most severe of all ecclesiastical punishments.[15] The personal interdict is removed only by absolution, which any confessor may impart, provided the interdict is not *ab homine* or reserved.[16]

Those bound by a personal interdict are, first of all, forbidden to celebrate or to assist at divine offices. Assistance at such offices may be considered either as active or as passive assistance. Thus, when a person participates in the divine offices by performing some office or duty,[17] the assistance is active. The assistance is passive when one merely attends the divine offices, or observes them by following what is done.[18]

Divine offices are sacred functions established by the institution of Christ, or of His Church, for the purpose of sacred worship, and can be performed only by those having the power of Orders.[19] Among the divine offices are the Holy Sacrifice of the Mass, the recitation of the Canonical Hours in choir, the blessing of water, candles, ashes, palms and the like. Consecrations must also be considered as divine offices; in other words, among the divine offices, are all sacred ceremonies ordained either by Christ or the Church for the purpose of sacred worship, and which can be performed only by clerics.[20] As is evident, there are many popular devotions, such as, for example, the public recitation of the Rosary and the Stations of the Cross,

---

14 Sole, *Ibidem.*

15 Sole, *Ibidem.*

16 Can. 2236, §1.

17 Cocchi, *Commentarium,* VIII, n. 87; Cheoldi, *Jus Poenale,* n. 37.

18 Hyland, *Excommunication,* p. 53.

19 Can. 2256, n. 1.

20 Sole, *op. cit.,* n. 202; Schmalzgrueber, Pars IV, tit. XXXIX, n. 361; Cappello, *De Censuris,* n. 149.

which do not constitute divine offices, at least in the technical sense of the term.[21]

Those under personal interdict in the time of the old law were forbidden to assist at divine offices. Thus, in granting a concession to the faithful in general, the Corpus Juris Canonici frequently employs the following restricting clause, "excommunicatis et interdictis exclusis." [22] The old law was quite rigorous in this regard, even to the extent that excommunicated and interdicted persons whose censure was publicly known were to be expelled from the celebration of Mass; otherwise it was necessary for the celebrant to desist.

Later, however, a distinction was made in the case of excommunicated persons, by virtue of which they were classified as either *tolerati* or *vitandi.* This distinction was introduced by Pope Martin V, in his Constitution *"Ad Evitanda,"* in 1418.[23] Accordingly, the faithful were no longer obliged to abstain *in sacris* with such excommunicated persons as were termed "tolerati." Although it is true that this distinction was introduced not for the sake of excommunicated persons, but for the benefit of the faithful, never-the less, accidentally, at least, the rigor of the old law relaxed in favor of certain excommunicated persons *(tolerati).* Exactly when the practice of expelling excommunicated persons known as *tolerati* ceased, is a matter of doubt. Moreover, the provision that excommunicated persons, including *tolerati,* should remain away from divine offices remained in force even after the time of Pope Martin V, and any violation of this regulation was considered serious.[24]

Unlike Canon 2259, §1, which, treating of the effects of excommunication, uses the phrase: *excommunicatus quili-*

---

21 Augustine, *Commentary,* VIII, 177.

22 C. 57, X, *de sent. excom.* V, 39: "Permittimus ecclesiarum ministros semel in hebdomada tempore interdicti, non pulsatis campanis, voce submissa, januis clausis, excommunicatis et interdictis exclusis, Missarum solemnia celebrare causa conficiendi Corpus Domini quod decedentibus in poenitentia non negatur."

23 *Fontes,* n. 45.

24 Hyland, *Excommunication,* p. 55.

bet caret jure assistendi divinis officiis, Canon 2275, n. 1, employs a very emphatic clause: *Personaliter interdicti nequeunt divina officia celebrare eisve,...assistere.* It is quite clear from the wording of this canon, that those under personal interdict are forbidden to assist at divine offices. The phrase *caret jure,* of Canon 2259, §1, does leave considerable doubt in the minds of authors as to whether excommunicated persons are strictly forbidden to attend divine offices, or whether they merely forfeit their right to assist.[25]

Although Canon 2275 is parallel to Canon 2259, nevertheless each of these Canons uses very different terminology in describing the discipline relative to attending divine offices. Canon 2259, §1, merely states that any excommunicated person is deprived of the right to assist at divine offices, while Canon 2275, n. 1, plainly states that personally interdicted persons cannot assist at them. From this, it seems that the former merely forfeits his right to assist at divine offices, while the latter are strictly forbidden to do so. This difference is, to say the least, quite surprising when one considers that excommunication is a more severe penalty than the personal interdict. It must be remembered, however, that it is the immediate purpose of the interdict to forbid the use of certain sacred things enumerated in the canons,[26] while the direct and immediate effect of excommunication is the separation of one of the faithful from the communion of his fellow-Christians; in the case of excommunicated persons, the use of sacred things is only indirectly forbidden, i.e., inasmuch the excommunicated person is placed outside the communion of the faithful, the natural consequence of which is the privation of the use of certain sacred things.[27]

The apparent severity of Canon 2275, n. 1, in comparison with Canon 2259, §1, may easily be explained by the fact that it is the direct and immediate purpose of the interdict to deprive the delinquent of certain sacred things; moreover,

---

[25] Hyland, *op. cit.*, p. 58 ff.

[26] Can. 2268.

[27] Can. 2257.

this end can be obtained in no better way than by forbidding him to attend Holy Mass and other divine offices.

It will be noticed that a twofold prohibition is contained in the first clause of Canon 2275, n. 1, namely: the personally interdicted are forbidden, (1) to celebrate divine offices; (2) to assist at divine offices. If, of course, assistance at divine office is denied to the personally interdicted, *a fortiori*, celebrating divine offices, which is the active assistance, must be forbidden.

The remarks immediately preceding have reference to the celebration and attendance on the part of interdicted persons at divine offices. There is one exception to this ruling, however, which has to do with attending sermons or the preaching of the word of God.

While yet in this world, Christ gave a special mandate to His Apostles and to their successors to preach the Gospel to every creature,[28] and, accordingly, the Church has always exercised the greatest care that even the most wayward should not be deprived of so salutary a blessing. To demonstrate the truth of this assertion, no better evidence can be produced than a canon of the fourth Council of Carthage, in 419: "*Episcopus nullum prohibeat ingredi ecclesiam, et audire verbum Dei, sive gentilem, sive hereticum sive Judaeum, usque ad Missam catechumenorum.*" [29] Likewise, when the Bishop of Ferrara asked whether he could lawfully gather together all the excommunicated and interdicted persons into a church each week for the purpose of preaching the Gospel to them, and thereby to effect their conversion, answer was given that he could do so without any qualms of conscience, as often as it was necessary, and as long as no divine office was actually celebrated during the preaching.[30] Moreover, as Vermeersch-Creusen [31] point out, oftentimes preaching the word of God is the last and only chance to bring the unruly, and especially such as are under censure, to a sense of duty.

[28] *Mark*, XVI, 15.

[29] C. 67, D. 1, *de consecr.*

[30] C. 43, X, *de sent. excom.*, V, 39.

[31] *Epitome*, III, 461.

The present attitude of the Church with regard to preaching the word of God to excommunicated and interdicted persons in no wise deviates from the discipline of the former legislation. Hence the Church neither deprives such persons of the right to attend the preaching of the word of God, and, much less, does she make a positive prohibition to this effect.

It is now necessary to determine exactly what is included in the expression *praedicatio verbi Dei.* The Code itself devotes an entire title to this matter.[32] Consequently, under the phrase *praedicatio verbi Dei* are included catechetical instructions, sermons and missions.

Must these sermons and instructions be entirely separated from all divine offices? It is the opinion of Cocchi [33] and Blat [34] that excommunicated and interdicted persons may attend instructions and sermons, even if they are held during Mass. This opinion, however, is difficult to sustain, if these authors mean to maintain that persons under excommunication or interdict may also attend the divine offices which precede or follow the preaching. Thus, Augustine [35] rightly remarks that assistance at sermons or instructions does not permit assistance at divine offices. Therefore, to state the matter briefly, those under personal interdict are forbidden to celebrate divine offices or to assist thereat, but in no wise are they forbidden to assist at the preaching of the word of God.

Passive assistentes non est necesse ut expellantur; sed ab assistentia activa, quae aliquam secumferat participationem in divinis officiis celebrandis, repellantur interdicti post latam sententiam condemnatoriam vel declaratoriam, aut alioquin notorie interdicti.

It will be remembered that the first clause in Canon 2275, n. 1, prohibits those under sentence of personal interdict to celebrate, or even to assist at divine offices, with the one and only exception of assisting at the preaching of the word

---

[32] Lib. III, tit. XX, Canons 1327-1351.

[33] *Commentarium,* V, n. 87.

[34] *Commentarium,* V, n. 86.

[35] *Commentary,* VIII, 177.

of God. Canon 2275, n. 1, further states that it is not necessary to expel personally interdicted persons who are passively assisting at divine services. It must be remembered that such persons are strictly forbidden to attend divine offices. In fact, the clause, *non est necesse ut expellantur,* implies that according to the strict application of the law, such persons may be expelled. But while they may be expelled, the reason for the milder mode of procedure is very probably to avoid the scandals which would otherwise result. Furthermore, it must also be remembered that, even were it mandatory to expel those under personal interdict, there would be great danger of publicly exposing another's delinquent state by such public expulsion. Accordingly, the Church pursues a prudent course in not demanding the expulsion of those under personal interdict while passively assisting at divine offices. Moreover, it is all too obvious that if the expulsion of such delinquents were put into practice, besides giving rise to much scandal, it would certainly result in the unwarranted and unnecessary revelation of the censure of an occult delinquent. It is to be admitted, of course, that the present discipline makes no distinction between occultly and publicly interdicted persons, but it is a recognized fact that public expulsion of personally interdicted individuals, whether public or occult, would certainly cause more harm than good. This is all the more likely because the legislation has reference to public divine offices, consequently expulsion from such functions is correspondingly public. Furthermore, since Canon 2275 is parallel to Canon 2259, which plainly states that tolerated excommunicated persons assisting passively at divine services need not be expelled, and since such persons are tolerated by the Church itself and by the faithful in general, *a pari,* the same toleration should be extended to those under sentence of personal interdict.

Vermeersch-Creusen, in treating Canon 2259, §1, make the following statement: "Ipsis Codicis verbis solvitur disputatio olim inter auctores vigens num excommunicato tolerato divinis assistere liceret." [36] Likewise, treating the

[36] *Epitome,* III, n. 461.

clause, *Si passive assistat toleratus non est necesse ut expellatur,* they state: "Confirmatur disciplina mitior quae jam a satis multis annis vigebat et praeclaros defensores habeat. Assistentia enim passiva divinis officiis, nisi in signum contemptus fiat, ad convertendos animos plurimum valet." [37] Likewise, Genicot, speaking of assistance of tolerated excommunicated persons, writes: "Assistentia divinis officiis non prohibita est excommunicatis toleratis.... Immo Ecclesia heterodoxos potius allicit ad officia sua frequentanda quam eos ab iisdem removet, cum hac frequentatione crebro ad conversionem adducantur." [38] Now if all the above-mentioned opinions obtain in favor of tolerated excommunicated persons, *a pari,* the same should be applied in the case of those under personal interdict, because the legislation of Canon 2259, §1, concerning the passive assistance of tolerated excommunicated persons, and the legislation of Canon 2275, n. 1, concerning the passive assistance of personally interdicted individuals, are identical.

Sed ab assistentia activa, quae aliquam secumferat participationem in divinis officiis celebrandis, repellantur interdicti post latam sententiam condemnatoriam vel declaratoriam, aut alioquin notorie interdicti.

In the section of Canon 2275, n. 1, which has just been quoted, an explanation is given of what is meant by *active assistance.* Thus, active assistance is that which comprises some participation in the celebration of divine offices.[39]

From this provision of Canon 2275, n. 1, it is clear that active assistance at divine offices is denied under penalty of expulsion to those under personal interdict, only after a condemnatory or declaratory sentence has been issued. Hence, by inference at least, it seems that active assistance cannot be denied personally interdicted individuals to the extent of expelling them, so long as no condemnatory or declaratory sentence has been pronounced. The objection might be raised that n. 1 of Canon 2275 merely tolerates personally interdicted individuals *passively* assisting at

---

[37] *Ibidem.*

[38] *Institutiones Theologiae Moralis,* 10. ed., II, n. 583.

[39] Sole, *De Delictis et Poenis,* n. 215.

divine offices, and, consequently, they must be expelled when there is question of *active assistance,* i.e., a participation in the divine offices. There is, however, no warrant for this objection, for it is the accepted principle of both Roman Law [40] and Canon Law,[41] that in penal discipline the milder interpretation is to be followed. Likewise, it is another provision of Canon Law [42] that laws which establish punishments, or which restrict the free exercise of rights, must be strictly interpreted. Bearing this in mind, one cannot help but admit that Canon 2275, n. 1, does not make a provision to expel interdicted persons taking active part in divine services before a condemnatory or declaratory sentence has been passed. The text is quite clear: "sed ab assistentia activa,. . .repellantur interdicti *post latam sententiam condemnatoriam vel declaratoriam.*" Accordingly, persons under personal interdict, after a condemnatory or declaratory sentence has been passed, are to be expelled from active assistance at divine offices. The obvious inference to be drawn from the foregoing is that *before a condemnatory or declaratory sentence has been passed,* personally interdicted individuals are not to be expelled from active assistance at divine offices, unless, of course, they are notoriously interdicted.

Once a condemnatory or declaratory sentence has been declared, or if the delinquent is notoriously interdicted, the obligation to expel him from active assistance at divine offices is grave.[43]

In the case of one who is notoriously interdicted, the same *modus agendi* is to be adopted as in the case of those whose censure of interdict has been made known by a declaratory or condemnatory sentence, i.e., one who is notoriously interdicted is to be expelled from active assistance at divine offices.[44] The obligation on the part of those conducting the divine services, to expel those who are notoriously

---

[40] *Reg.* 15, 49, R. J., in VI°.

[41] Can. 2219, §1.

[42] Can. 19.

[43] Vermeersch-Creusen, *Epitome,* III, n. 477; Can. 2338, §3.

[44] Vermeersch-Creusen, *Epitome,* III, n. 477.

interdicted, is, according to Vermeersch-Creusen,[45] a grave one.

Although the Code makes it obligatory to expel, from active participation in divine offices, all interdicted persons against whom a condemnatory or declaratory sentence has been passed, together with all those whose censure of interdict is otherwise publicly known, nevertheless no instructions are given in the Code itself as to the mode of procedure to be employed in fulfilling this obligation. It seems likely that a warning to leave the church would be sufficient. In former times, if such a warning went unheeded physical force was employed wherever it was possible.[46]

It is likely, however, that the grave inconvenience which would arise in the event of the delinquent's refusal to depart, and the further inconvenience which would arise in attempting to use physical force, would be sufficient to excuse one from enforcing this law, which, after all, is of ecclesiastical origin. In most countries, where it is the custom of the civil authorities to protect and guard any group of citizens gathered in an act of worship, there is little possibility of difficulty in this matter. If, therefore, the delinquent refused to leave the church upon warning, and created any disorder, the matter could easily be settled by seeking the aid of the civil authorities.[47]

Unlike the provisions of Canon 2259, §2, which orders the service to be discontinued if the *vitandus* refuses to leave, Canon 2275, n. 1, makes no such demand. The absence of this demand leads one to conclude that the obligation to expel a notoriously interdicted person is not as grave as that of expelling a notoriously excommunicated person. The Church must judge the necessity of expelling a notoriously excommunicated person as an extremely grave one, when she demands that it be satisfied even to the extent of discontinuing the divine offices.

---

[45] *Ibidem.*

[46] Hyland, *Excommunication,* p. 66.

[47] Can. 2198.

Much has been said about divine offices. Much has also been said about active and passive assistance at divine offices. Consideration has been given to the legislation of the Church which excluded notoriously interdicted persons from active assistance at these divine offices. Exactly what active assistance is, may be deduced from the clause, *quae aliquam secumferat participationem in celebrandis divinis officiis.*[48] Now, one may be considered as assisting actively at divine offices, not only when he officiates in the capacity of celebrant, but even when he acts in certain subordinate capacities, such as, assistant priest, deacon, subdeacon, master of ceremonies, acolyte, and also as Mass server[49]

There is considerable doubt as to whether an organist may be considered as participating actively in divine offices.[50] It is the opinion of Chelodi[51] that the organist does not assist actively. Augustine,[52] however, contends that the organist participates actively in divine offices. In fact, it seems rather difficult to understand how an organist can be considered as merely passively assisting, when he seems so necessary in the conducting of solemn services. In like manner, it is the opinion of authors,[53] that singing or chanting in the choir during divine offices is to be considered as active participation. The reason for this apparent severity is that the definition of active assistance as given in the Canon is very wide in its embrace, and is to be understood in a wide sense.

II.—The Administration and Celebration of Sacraments and Sacramentals

According to Canon 2275, n. 2, those under personal interdict are forbidden not only to receive Sacraments and Sacra-

[48] Sole, *De Delictis et Poenis*, n. 215.

[49] Chelodi, *Jus Poenale*, n. 37, not. 4; Augustine, *Commentary*, VIII, 177; Cappello *De Censuris*, n. 149.

[50] Cappello, *op. cit.*, n. 149.

[51] *Jus Poenale*, n. 37, not. 4.

[52] *Commentary*, VIII, 177.

[53] Augustine, *op. cit.*, VIII, 177; Chelodi, *Jus Poenale*, n. 37, not. 4; Cappello, *De Censuris*, n. 149.

mentals according to the legislation of Canon 2260, §1, but are also forbidden to celebrate or administer Sacraments and Sacramentals according to the provisions of Canon 2261. This last-mentioned Canon, therefore, is parallel to Canon 2275, n. 2.

Canon 2261 states that an excommunicated person and, consequently, a personally interdicted individual, cannot licitly celebrate or administer Sacraments and Sacramentals, with due regard, however, for the exceptions which are to follow. The canon does not specify any Sacraments or Sacramentals in particular, and, therefore, the general rule refers to all the Sacraments.

Since there is a prohibition not only against administering Sacraments but also against celebrating them, it is clear that a priest under a personal interdict cannot licitly celebrate the Holy Sacrifice of the Mass. Nor is this legislation of the Code an innovation, for the law in the time of the Decretals was equally strict: "Clerici autem qui a suis, aut etiam de mandato Romani Pontificis ab alienis episcopis interdicti vel excommunicati fuerint, et ante absolutionem divina officia celebraverint, nisi moniti sine dilatione redierint, perpetuae depositionis sententiam pro ausu tantae temeritatis incurrant." [54] It must be carefully borne in mind that this prohibitive law of the Church concerns obviously only the licit administration and celebration of the Sacraments. Therefore, if a priest, for instance, under a personal interdict, defiantly celebrated Mass, although he would certainly sin gravely, nevertheless the Mass would be a valid sacrifice. Nor should this seem surprising, because the Sacraments were so instituted by Christ that their valid administration depends on the proper placing of the matter and form together with the intention of doing what the Church does, and not upon the absence or presence of censures. The Sacrament of Penance, however, is an exception, because for the valid administration of this Sacrament, the power of Orders alone does not suffice, but the power of jurisdiction is also necessary. The Church can, therefore, by withdrawing the power of jurisdiction

---

[54] C. 3, X, *de clerico excommunicato, deposito vel interdicto*, V, 27.

from unworthy ministers, render the valid administration of the Sacrament impossible. This the Church actually does in the case of *excommunicati vitandi*, and other excommunicated persons against whom a declaratory or condemnatory sentence has been passed.[55] To state the matter briefly, the power of jurisdiction can be taken away by a censure, but the power of orders can in no wise be taken away.

Concerning the valid administration of Sacramentals, Cappello writes: "Attamen dubitandum non est, quin ecclesia cujus omnimodae potestati subsunt sacramentalia, posset, absolute loquendo, vetare etiam *sub poena nullitatis* ne clericus excommunicatus (idem dicas de suspenso vel interdicto) sacramentalia conficeret aut ministrat." [56] All will admit that the Church, upon which the efficacy of Sacramentals depends, certainly has the power to forbid those under personal interdict to administer or celebrate them under pain of nullity; nevertheless, it cannot be deduced from the wording of the canons that it is her intention to do so. It seems safe to conclude, therefore, that the celebration or administration of Sacramentals by those under personal interdict, although unlawful, is nevertheless valid.

Thus far, consideration has been given to the law of the Code which forbids those under personal interdict to celebrate and administer Sacraments and Sacramentals. Consideration must now be given to the exception from the general provision of Canon 2261. The intention of the Church in depriving interdicted persons of the right to administer Sacraments and Sacramentals might be said to be twofold: (1) to protect sacred things from desecration and (2) to punish the delinquent, thereby bringing him to the consideration of the gravity of his delict, and, ultimately, to bring about his conversion and reconciliation to the Church. But, while the Church wishes to deprive the unworthy of the right to administer Sacraments and Sacramentals, she certainly does not wish to do so to the extent of making it impossible or seriously inconvenient for the

---

[55] Can. 2264.

[56] *De Censuris*, n. 48.

faithful to receive them. It is for this reason, therefore, and for this reason only, that the Church modifies the strict law of forbidding interdicted persons to administer Sacraments and Sacramentals. The one and only intention of the Church in mitigating this law is to favor her worthy children; consequently, any favor which the unworthy may enjoy is purely accidental or circumstantial. The Church certainly does not wish that the spiritual welfare of the faithful should be endangered merely because of the unworthiness of those who are ordained to administer the Sacraments.

According to the law of the Decretals,[57] the administration of Sacraments by a censured person would be licit by reason of ignorance in the minister. It must be carefully borne in mind that there is question here of *licit* administration. If, notwithstanding the prohibitive law, a censured person administered Sacraments, the administration would indeed be valid, save in the case of Penance. A censured minister who knowingly violated the law by administering Sacraments not only sinned gravely but even incurred new penalties.[58] Likewise, the Constitution, "Apostolicae Sedis" of Pope Pius IX, stated that anyone who received a Sacred Order from an excommunicate who was a *vitandus,* was by that very fact suspended from exercising the Order received.

The second and third paragraphs of Canon 2261 (which legislate for interdicted as well as for excommunicated persons) state the exception from the general rule which forbids censured persons to administer Sacraments and Sacramentals. Thus, it is provided in §2 of Canon 2261, that the faithful, with due regard for the ruling of §3 of this Canon, for any just cause, may ask an excommunicated minister to administer the Sacraments and Sacramentals, especially if no other minister is present; moreover, when the excommunicate is asked to do so, he may administer the Sacraments or Sacramentals, and he is not obliged to inquire into the reasons of the one desiring to receive them.

---

[57] C. 9, X, *de clerico excommunicato,* V, 27.

[58] C. 10, X, *de clerico excommunicato,* V, 27.

It can readily be seen that the most frequently occurring reason for requesting an interdicted minister to administer the Sacraments would be the absence of other ministers. The reason just mentioned, however, seems to be more than a mere just cause; for if there is a necessity or even a strong desire on the part of one of the faithful to receive a Sacrament, and no other priest is present to officiate, there certainly would seem to be a grave reason for asking a censured priest to administer the Sacrament. But it is not necessary that there be a grave reason; the canon merely demands a just cause. In this connection, Vermeersch-Creusen write: "Justa, non gravis, causa requiritur, qualis est maturior Baptismi collatio, dubium de gravitate peccati deponendum, intentio cum majori animi puritate ad Synaxim accedendi, intentio etiam saepius communicandi, etc." [59] Augustine [60] declares that any cause may be considered just which really enhances devotion, or which is prompted by a real convenience, for instance, if one does not want to call another minister. Concerning this matter, Cerato writes: "*Immo etiam implicita* fidelium petitio ab illiceitate excusaret; et sic parochus vel cappellanus, etsi excommunicatione occulta impediti sint, *licite* sistent die dominica in templo parati ad fidelium confessiones, uti solent diebus dominicis, excipiendas, ad Missam pro populo celebrandam ceteraque Sacramenta administranda." [61] Vermeersch-Creusen further remark: "Petitio ex parte fidelium *implicita* sufficit. Ita cum plures singulis sabbatis et, mane, diebus dominicis sacramentum poenitentiae recipere soleant et in hebdomada communicare, sacerdos praesertim occulta excommunicatione irretitus, ad audiendas confessiones vel distribuendam S. Communionem se paratum sponte ostendere potest." [62]

From the above quotations, it follows that the faithful should have no scruples when there is an occasion to request a minister who is under personal interdict to admin-

---

[59] *Epitome,* III, n. 463.

[60] *Commentary,* VIII, 182.

[61] *Censurae Vigentes,* p. 60.

[62] *Ibidem.*

ister Sacraments and Sacramentals. Attention must be given, however, to the phrase, "maxime si alii ministri desint," which seems to imply that the faithful have an obligation at least in charity to avoid, without too great an inconvenience, leading another into sin.[63] It is clear that if the interdicted minister celebrated or administered a Sacrament without first eliciting an act of perfect sorrow for his sin, he would undoubtedly commit a sacrilege.

Therefore, the general provision regarding those under excommunication and personal interdict is that they are forbidden to celebrate or administer Sacraments and Sacramentals. The general principle is stated in §1 of Canon 2261. An exception to this general principle is stated in §2 of the same Canon. A restriction of this exception is made in §3 which states that when there is question of *excommunicati vitandi,* or of other excommunicated persons against whom a condemnatory or declaratory sentence has been passed, only the faithful who are in danger of death may seek sacramental absolution, according to the provisions of Canons 882 and 2252 from such excommunicates; and then if other ministers are not present, the faithful (in danger of death) may also ask them to administer other Sacraments and Sacramentals. It will be remembered that in the exception contained in §2 of Canon 2261, there was question of *excommunicati tolerati,* and, consequently, of interdicted persons against whom no declaratory or condemnatory sentence has been passed, or whose censure is not otherwise notorious. The question naturally arises as to when, or under what circumstances, may the faithful seek the administration of Sacraments and Sacramentals from a notoriously interdicted person, or from one against whom a declaratory or condemnatory sentence has been passed. The answer is quite clear from the wording of the Code; accordingly, such persons may be called to administer Sacraments and Sacramentals only in the case when one of the faithful is in danger of death; moreover, they are then free to ask for sacramental absolution only according to the provisions of Canons 882 and 2252; lastly,

---

[63] Vermeersch-Creusen, *ibidem.*

the faithful may ask for the administration of other Sacraments and Sacramentals, provided no other ministers are present to administer them.

It seems necessary at this point to determine exactly what is meant by the term *periculum mortis*. One may be said to be in danger of death if there is a prudent fear or real probability that he will die. It must be carefully borne in mind that the Code does not require *articulum mortis*, which is had when death is imminent, or when the person is actually said to be dying. D'Annibale states that *periculum mortis* signifies "illud rerum discrimen in quo, cum quis constitutus est, ipsum et superesse et occumbere posse, utrumque est vere graviterque probabile." [64] *Periculum mortis* means that there is a probability of death. This probability of death must be understood reasonably, in accordance with the mind of the Church.[65] Therefore, a man may be in probable danger of death even if his recovery is really probable.[66] Consequently, there is no necessity that the person in whose favor the privilege is to be used should be in *articulo mortis;* it is required and suffices that the danger of death be such that there is still a probable chance that death will not ensue. This danger may arise from various causes. The cause may be intrinsic, i.e., sickness, infirmity caused by old age, or a wound; on the other hand, the cause may be extrinsic, e.g., in the case of soldiers about to go into battle, also major operations and dangerous voyages.[67] In the case of a positive doubt as to whether or not the person is really constituted in danger of death, it seems that the benefit of the doubt must be given in favor of the person seeking the Sacraments; for it is stated in Canon 209 that in a positive and probable doubt, the Church supplies jurisdiction for both the internal and external forum. From this it is clear that even in the case where a priest administers Sacraments on the supposition that the person was in danger, when in fact there was no

---

[64] *Summa Theologia Moralis*, I, n. 38.

[65] Kilker, *Extreme Unction*, p. 167.

[66] Genicot, *Institutiones Theologiae Moralis*, II, n. 422.

[67] Hyland, *Excommunication*, p. 94.

danger of death at all, such administration would be both valid and licit.

Only when one of the faithful is in danger of death may he ask sacramental absolution from a personally interdicted priest against whom a declaratory or condemnatory sentence has been passed. It will be remembered that the Sacrament of Penance differs from the other Sacraments in so far as its valid administration requires more than the power of Orders; the power of Jurisdiction is also necessary. The Ordinary may withdraw this power of Jurisdiction from one of his priests for any good reason. Thus, when a priest is under sentence of personal interdict, and a condemnatory or declaratory sentence has been passed against him, he loses his jurisdiction for the hearing of confessions.[68] Therefore it is evident that if a priest so interdicted attempts to hear confessions (save when asked to do so by one in danger of death) the absolution imparted by him would certainly be invalid. It will be remembered that in the case of other Sacraments, such jurisdiction is not required; therefore if an interdicted priest against whom a sentence has been passed, administers Baptism or celebrates Mass, although he would be sinning gravely, nevertheless he would act validly. But when there is question of the Sacrament of Penance, a priest is unable to act validly once his power of Jurisdiction has been withdrawn. Of course, when there is extreme necessity, the Church itself supplies such priests with jurisdiction. Thus, it is provided in Canon 882 that when there is danger of death, all priests, although not approved for hearing confessions, may, nevertheless, validly and licitly grant absolution to all penitents from all sins and censures in whatever manner they may be reserved, even if another priest approved for the hearing of confessions is present; due regard, however, must be had for the provisions of Canons 884 and 2252.

The faculty granted in Canon 882 is somewhat restricted by Canon 884 wherein it is stated: "Absolutio complicis in peccato turpi invalida est, praeterquam in mortis periculo; et etiam in mortis periculo, extra casum necessitatis, est ex

---

[68] Can. 873, §3.

parte confessarii illicita ad norman constitutionum apostolicarum et nominatim constitutionis Benedicti XIV *Sacramentum Poenitentiae,* 1 Jun. 1741." Therefore, with the one exception just mentioned, an interdicted priest, even though a condemnatory or declaratory sentence has been passed, may, nevertheless, validly and licitly absolve all persons in danger of death, even if another priest approved for the hearing of confessions is present. The Church wishes to grant every possible convenience to all her children, and especially to those constituted in danger of death. Hence, she does not state that a *post sententiam* interdicted priest can impart sacramental absolution only when no other priest is present; the Church, realizing the great necessity of the Sacrament of Penance, allows such a priest to impart sacramental absolution even if other priests are present who enjoy the power of jurisdiction and are free from all censures.

The reason for such magnanimity on the part of the Church is to grant every possible liberty to the dying in choosing a confessor. All will certainly admit that a priest duly approved for hearing confessions is to be preferred to one notoriously censured. Moreover, the cases in which one of the faithful in danger of death would insist on the ministrations of a notoriously interdicted priest would be extremely rare. Nevertheless, the Church, in her ardent desire to enhance the salvation of souls, provides for every possible contingency; hence if the faithful desire to confess to such priests as are in question, as long as there is danger of death, they may do so.

An interdicted priest who administers Sacraments and Sacramentals, according to §2 and §3 of Canon 2261, acts both validly and licitly. It is a question here, of course, of liceity by reason of censure and not by reason of sin. In this connection, Sole writes: "Diximus, *licite ratione censurae,* idest excommunicati, in casibus praedictis, Sacramenta ministrando ad normam §2 et §3, non peccant contra censuram excommunicationis. Secus enim lex sibi ipsi contradiceret; quia dum ex una parte permitteretur fidelibus petere ab excommunicato Sacramenta et Sacramentalia, ex alia parte, saltem indirecte, ratione caritatis, huiusmodi petitio Sacramentorum prohibeatur."[69] In like manner Cerato remarks: "Licite, inquam, ratione *censurae;* etenim ratione *delicti,* quod non deterserint Sacramento Poenitentiae vel saltem, si copia defuerit confessarii, actu contritionis, illicite profecto agerent."[70]

It is to be noted that the provision of Canon 2252 must be kept in mind in reference to the permission granted in §3 of Canon 2261. It is provided in Canon 2252 that when a penitent who is in danger of death is absolved either from an *ab homine* censure or one which is reserved to the Holy See *specialissimo modo,* by a priest who does not enjoy special faculties, the penitent is obliged, after he has recovered his health, to have recourse to the superior who imposed the censure; or if the censure is reserved *specialissimo modo* to the Holy See, the recourse is to be made to the Sacred Penitentiary. The reason for such recourse is to receive and obey the mandates imposed. This obligation of making recourse directly affects the penitent and only indirectly affects the confessor. "Onus recurrendi ipsum paenitentem directe afficit, non confessarium, sed etiam *per confessarium* qui hoc onus suscipere debet, nisi gravi incommodo excusetur."[71]

It has been related how and under what conditions a *post sententiam* interdicted priest may impart sacramental absolution.[72] Even though a priest is censured in this manner, when the faithful are in danger of death, they may call on him for the purpose of confessing and obtaining absolution. The great anxiety of the Church for the salvation of souls is undoubtedly the purpose for so great a concession. It is to be kept in mind that the faithful may call upon a priest so interdicted for the purpose of obtaining absolution, even if other priests enjoying faculties and free from censures, are present. But such liberty is not granted to interdicted priests (after a declaratory or con-

---

[69] *De Delictis et Poenis,* n. 220.

[70] *Censurae Vigentes,* n. 37.

[71] Vermeersch-Creusen, *Epitome,* III, n. 452.

[72] Can. 2261, §3.

demnatory sentence has been passed), when there is question of the administration of other Sacraments and Sacramentals. Thus, the faithful, even though they be in danger of death, may ask a *post sententiam* interdicted priest to administer other Sacraments and Sacramentals only in the case when other ministers free from censure are present. The wording of the Code is quite exact in this matter; therefore many of the doubts which existed before the Code have been cleared up.

It was indeed but natural that doubt should arise as to which Sacraments a *post sententiam* interdicted priest could administer to the dying, when the legislation itself was not clear in the matter. Thus, Schmalzgrueber, treating the question of the valid and licit administration of Sacraments by excommunicates, writes: "Idem excommunicatus in eadem extrema necessitate potest periclitanti conferre sacramentum Baptismi; quia his omnibus necessarius est. De ceteris sacramentis, praesertim Eucharistiae, et Extremae Unctionis controvertunt DD. Satis convenit inter eosdem, Eucharistiam, vel Extremam Unctionem posse, et debere conferri etiam ab excommunicato in eo articulo, quando moribundus Sacramentum Poenitentiae non potest suscipere."[73] Furthermore, it was quite logical for pre-Code authors to hold that Extreme Unction should be given in cases in which the dying person could not make his confession. With regard to the administration of the other Sacraments by a *post sententiam* interdicted or excommunicated minister, it was the opinion of Saint Alphonsus [74] that the Holy Eucharist could be administered. His opinion was based on the fact that, although this Sacrament was not a *sine qua non* condition for salvation, nevertheless it was so extremely useful for the dying person in his last battle for salvation, that it seemed but natural to take for granted that the Church wished him to benefit by so great an aid. The administration of the other Sacraments, however, on the part of a notoriously interdicted or ex-

---

[73] Pars IV, tit., XXXIX, n. 145.

[74] *Theologia Moralis*, VI, n. 88.

communicated minister was strictly forbidden according to the opinion of most pre-code authors.[75]

Since the promulgation of the Code, there is really but slight possibility of any doubt in this matter. The wording is so clear that one can readily discern what is permitted and what is forbidden. When the faithful are in danger of death, they may ask an interdicted priest (after a declaratory or condemnatory sentence) to impart sacramental absolution. This they may do even when other priests free from censures are present. Beyond this, the faithful in danger of death may ask a priest so interdicted to administer other Sacraments and Sacramentals only when no other priests are present. A *post sententiam* interdicted priest, administering Sacraments and Sacramentals under the circumstances just mentioned, administers them both validly and licitly.

Although the Code states that the dying person must ask for the administration of the Sacraments and Sacramentals in order that a *post sententiam* interdicted priest may administer them licitly (by reason of the censure), nevertheless, it does not seem that the asking must be explicit. Thus, Vermeersch-Creusen, treating this matter, write: "Petitio ex parte fidelium *implicita sufficit.*" [76] Therefore if one of the faithful who have lived a true Christian life is in danger of death, and is also already destitute of his senses, it certainly is reasonable to presume that such a person would certainly ask a *post sententiam* interdicted priest to administer the Sacraments, if no other priests were present. Moreover, when the dying person is unconscious, and, therefore, unable to confess his sins, it certainly is the mind of the Church that such a person should receive Extreme Unction at all costs, because under such circumstances the salvation of the dying person's soul may be dependent upon the administration of the Sacrament of Extreme Unction. Therefore, if a dying Catholic person is already destitute of his senses, a priest who is interdicted by a sentence should

---

[75] Schmalzgrueber, *loc. cit.;* Reiffenstuel, lib. V, tit. XXXIX, n. 203.

[76] *Epitome,* III, n. 463.

have no hesitancy in administering Extreme Unction or any Sacramental which is useful to the dying person, if no other priest is present to do so.

III.—The Reception of Sacraments and Sacramentals

Prohibentur Sacramenta et Sacramentalia. . .recipere, ad normam can. 2260, §1.

Besides the prohibition against the administration of Sacraments and Sacramentals by those under personal interdict, Canon 2275, n. 2, also forbids such persons to receive the Sacraments and Sacramentals according to the provision of Canon 2260, §1.

It will be remembered that the general purpose of the personal interdict is to deprive those bound by it of certain spiritual benefits. Now, among the many and varied benefits which a Christian enjoys, there is none greater than the Sacraments, which are the very channels through which the grace of God flows to us. It is not surprising, therefore, that the Church should deprive those under the ban of personal interdict of participation in these great benefits.

During the time of local interdict, whether particular or general, only certain Sacraments are prohibited,[77] but when there is question of those under personal interdict, the same regulations obtain as for those under the censure of excommunication. The wording of the Canon does not specify any particular Sacraments; it simply states that personally interdicted persons are forbidden to receive the Sacraments and Sacramentals in exactly the same measure as excommunicates are deprived of them according to Canon 2260, §1. It is evident, therefore, that those under personal interdict are on the same level as excommunicated persons, as far as the reception of Sacraments is concerned. Consequently it will be necessary to examine the legislation concerning excommunicated persons in this matter.

Canon 2260, §1, makes the statement that an excommunicated person may not receive the Sacraments;

[77] Can. 2270, §1.

moreover, after a declaratory or condemnatory sentence, he is forbidden to receive Sacramentals.

As a natural sequel of excommunication, the reception of the Sacraments was forbidden to those under its ban. This discipline is in no wise changed by the legislation contained in the Code.[78] The prudence of this legislation is obvious; for, one who obdurately refuses to listen to the dictates of the Church is reasonably denied the right of participating in her greatest and most singular benefits. Moreover, both excommunication and the interdict are medicinal penalties, the primary end of which is to restore the delinquent to a sense of duty and decency. This end can be realized in no better way than by denying those under the ban the privilege of receiving the Sacraments.[79]

Now if all this be true in regard to excommunication, which, after all, denies the Sacraments to those under its ban only as a *consequence*, it can easily be understood why the same is true with regard to the censure of interdict, the direct aim of which is to deprive the delinquent of the use of spiritual goods and benefits. And who will deny that among these spiritual goods and benefits the Sacraments are the greatest? For the Sacraments are the normal channels through which the grace of God is transmitted to us; they are the means whereby Christians share the fruits of the Redemption. If all this be true, it is not difficult to understand why the privation of the Sacraments is so serious a matter.

It is stated in Canon 2260, §1, that an excommunicated person cannot receive the Sacraments, and, consequently, the same discipline obtains for those under personal interdict.[80] A controversy might easily enough arise as to whether reference is here made concerning the valid reception of the Sacraments or their licit reception, since Canon 2260, §1, does not employ the term *licite*. It seems quite obvious that in this connection there is question of licit reception of the Sacraments and not of the validity of their

[78] C. 32, X, *de sent. excom.*, V, 39; C. 24, *de sent. excom.*, V, in VI°.

[80] Can. 2275, n. 2.

[79] Sole, *De Delictis et Poenis*, n. 216.

reception. It is true that Canon 2261, §1, in speaking of the prohibition against administering Sacraments and Sacramentals on the part of an excommunicate, employs the term *licite*. Very likely the Code does not use the term *licite* in Canon 2260, §1, because the Sacraments are such that their reception can scarcely be invalidated by an ecclesiastical censure. Thus, a Sacrament received by an excommunicate or a personally interdicted person is *per se valid*, even if the recipient be in bad faith.[81] It must be carefully borne in mind, however, that if one under personal interdict attempts to receive the Sacrament of Penance, while conscious of his censure, his confession is not only illicit but even invalid. The reason for this is clear: if one attempts to receive absolution from his sins through sacramental confession before he obtains absolution from his censure, certainly his confession is invalid not because of his censure directly, but because in failing to obtain absolution from his censure he lacks the necessary conditions, and, consequently, is indisposed to receive the Sacrament. Cappello [82] states that this invalidity is due not to the censure but to the lack of proper disposition in the penitent himself. In this connection, Sole remarks: "Quamvis illicite, valide tamen excommunicati recipiunt Sacramenta, dummodo excipiatur Sacramentum Poenitentiae mala fide susceptum." [83] Sole [84] further states that the validity of a Sacrament depends on the institution of Christ, and cannot be impeded by an ecclesiastical censure.

It can be said, therefore, that *per se* a personally interdicted individual cannot licitly receive any Sacrament unless he first obtains absolution from the censure. Therefore, he gravely sins who, while bound by a personal interdict, dares to receive a Sacrament, unless he is excused by some extenuating cause, such as invincible ignorance, fear of

---

81 Hyland, *Excommunication*, p. 75.

82 *De Censuris*, n. 147.

83 *De Delictis et Poenis*, n. 217; cfr. etiam Schmalzgrueber, Pars IV, tit. XXXIX, n. 140.

84 *Ibidem*.

death or of infamy;[85] for the laws of the Church do not bind under such grave inconveniences.

Notwithstanding all that has been said concerning the prohibition to receive Sacraments on the part of those under personal interdict, it is only because of positive obstinacy and open contempt that a delinquent is really deprived of the Sacraments.[86] The truth of this statement is sufficiently demonstrated by the Code itself which gives to confessors very extensive faculties of absolving from censures, according as different necessities arise. Thus Canon 882 authorizes all priests, whether approved for hearing confessions or not, to absolve validly and licitly any penitent in danger of death from any sin or censure, even if another priest is present who is approved for the hearing of confessions; however, the provisions laid down in Canons 884 and 2252 must be understood in connection with this faculty. That the Church is willing to show kindness and consideration even towards delinquents is shown in Canon 2254, which gives confessors special faculties to absolve from censures in unusually urgent cases. For, according to this Canon, confessors are authorized to absolve from a *latae sententiae* censure when the same cannot be observed in the external forum without grave scandal, or without jeopardizing the reputation of the individual under censure; likewise, confessors have the same authority to absolve from *latae sententiae* censures when it would be a real hardship for the censured person to remain under the ban while faculties are being sought from a competent Superior. When may it be said that the otherwise necessary delay is a hardship to the penitent? In general, this is largely to be judged from the disposition of the penitent in each individual case.[87] It is the opinion of Sole [88] that it may also be considered a hardship for the penitent to remain under the censure for a single day. It is really necessary that the penitent experience a hardship, but the

[85] Sole, *op. cit.*, n. 216.

[86] Cerato, *Censurae Vigentes*, n. 37.

[87] Cappello, *De Censuris*, n. 124.

[88] *De Delictis et Poenis*, n. 193.

confessor, in trying to dispose his penitent, may encourage these feelings.[89] When the confessor has no special faculties, the *recursus* is necessary, even in danger of death when there is question of *ab homine* censures or those which are *specialissimo modo* reserved to the Holy See. Therefore, it can easily be seen that the Church exercises every care, and exerts every means in order to afford all delinquents ample opportunity to reconcile themselves to their Mother, the Church.

It has been demonstrated that a personally interdicted person is forbidden to receive the Sacraments. From this fact it is clear that there rests with priests a corresponding obligation of denying the Sacraments to such persons. If priests are to be true to their calling as ministers of Christ and dispensers of the mysteries of God, they must do all in their power to protect holy things. *Sancta sancte tractanda sunt.* The Code itself makes a provision whereby unworthy persons, who are publicly known as such, are forbidden to receive Holy Communion.[90] Moreover, the principles of Moral Theology must come in for consideration here. Thus, if a person's unworthiness is not publicly known, he must not be denied the Sacraments if he seeks them publicly, but he must be denied them if he seeks them in secret.[91]

It is, and has been, the mind of the Church to do all in her power to prevent unworthy persons from receiving the Sacraments. Thus, the law in the time of the Decretals established severe punishments for those who administered Sacraments to the unworthy.[92] Likewise, the Constitution, "Apostolicae Sedis" of Pope Pius IX, confirmed this discipline:

> Scienter celebrantes vel celebrari facientes divina in locis ab Ordinario, vel delegato Judice, vel a jure interdictis, aut nomiatim excommunicatos ad divina officia, seu ecclesiastica Sacramenta, vel ecclesiasticam sepul-

---

[89] Cappello, *De Censuris*, n. 124.

[90] Can. 855, §1 and §2.

[91] Genicot-Salsmans, *Institutiones Theologiae Moralis*, 10 ed., II, n. 122.

[92] C. 8, *de priv.*, V, 7, in VI°.

> turam admittentes, interdictum ab ingressu Ecclesiae ipso jure incurrunt, donec ad arbitrium ejus, cujus sententiam contempserunt, competenter satisfecerint.[93]

From the above quotation, it can be clearly seen that the celebrated Constitution of Pius IX upheld the former discipline which was calculated to safeguard the Sacraments against unworthy and sacrilegious recipients. Nor does the legislation of the Code depart from the old discipline in this regard. Thus, the new law provides that ministers who dare to administer the Sacraments to such as are forbidden by either divine or ecclesiastical law to receive them, should be suspended by the Ordinary according to his own prudent judgment.[94] From this, it is clear that there is a serious obligation incumbent upon priests to prevent as far as possible unworthy persons from desecrating the Sacraments. Likewise, Canon 731, §2, states that it is forbidden to administer the Sacraments of the Church to heretics and schismatics, even if they be in good faith.

According to the legislation of Canon 2275, n. 2, those under the ban of personal interdict are forbidden to receive not only the Sacraments, but after a declaratory or condemnatory sentence, even the Sacramentals.[95] The Code itself gives us a definition of Sacramentals: "Sacramentalia sunt res aut actiones quibus Ecclesia, in aliquam Sacramentorum imitationem, uti solet ad obtinendos ex sua impetratione effectus praesertim spirtuales." [96] It will be noticed that Sacramentals differ from the Sacraments (1) by reason of their origin, i.e., all the Sacraments were instituted by Jesus Christ Himself, while the Sacramentals were instituted by the Church; (2) the Sacraments give grace *ex opere operato*, i.e., they give grace of themselves as long as the recipient places no obstacle in the way; while the Sacramentals give grace *ex opere operantis*, i.e., according to the disposition of the supporting prayer of the Church.[97]

---

[93] *Fontes*, n. 552.

[94] Can. 2364.

[95] Can. 2260, §1.

[96] Can. 1144.

[97] Tanquerey, *Synopsis Theologiae Dogmaticae*, 19 ed., III, n. 378; Vermeersch-Creusen, *Epitome*, II, n. 463.

A Sacramental is called a *res* when a certain object or thing is employed to cause the spiritual effect; among Sacramentals of this kind, are holy water, blessed ashes, blessed candles and the like. A Sacramental is an *actio* when certain actions are performed whereby the spiritual effect is produced.

Concerning the pre-Code legislation in this regard, it is rather difficult to trace any direct prohibition against the use of Sacramentals on the part of those under personal interdict. In this connection, Crnica writes: "Quid attinet autem ad Sacramentalia, in fontibus juris antiqui de ipsis nihil statutum est." [98]

From the wording of Canon 2260, §1, which legislates for both excommunicated and interdicted persons, it is clear that not all interdicted persons are necessarily deprived of the use of Sacramentals, but only such persons whose censure of interdict is publicly known by reason of a declaratory or condemnatory sentence.

A question may arise as to whether the reception of a Sacramental in defiance to the prohibition of Canon 2260, §1, is illicit only, or invalid also. It seems on the one hand that, since the efficacy of the Sacramentals depends on the supporting prayer of the Church, personally interdicted individuals are forbidden to receive them under the pain of nullity after a declaratory or condemnatory sentence has been passed. This seems all the more likely when it is remembered that the Church, upon which the efficacy of Sacramentals depends, prohibits such a person from receiving them. Furthermore, it would seem very contradictory to state that the Church wishes a person to benefit by the Sacramentals, and, at the same time, forbids the same person to receive them. Notwithstanding all that has been said above, it must also be kept in mind that, since Canon 2260, §1, makes no mention of invalidity concerning the reception of Sacramentals, and since in penal matters the milder interpretation is to be followed, the sentence favoring the validity of the reception of Sacramentals by those under personal interdict has intrinsic probability.

---

[98] *Modificationes in Tract. de Cen.*, p. 93.

Inasmuch as exorcisms come under the heading of Sacramentals, it seems necessary to make mention of them here. The very nature and purpose of exorcisms seem to demand that they be performed in favor of anyone who needs them. Accordingly, the Code specifically states that the legitimate ministers may perform them not only upon the faithful and catechumens, but also upon non-Catholics and excommunicated persons.[99] Now, although Canon 1152 makes no mention of interdicted persons, nevertheless it is evidently the implicit intention of the legislator to include them. What is said in favor of excommunicated persons, *a pari* applies to those under personal interdict. Furthermore, Canon 2275, n. 2, declares that those under personal interdict are forbidden to administer, celebrate and receive Sacraments and Sacramentals in exactly the same degree as excommunicated persons are forbidden to administer, celebrate or receive them. Moreover, this is all the more probable since even *excommunicati vitandi* are included in Canon 1152.[100] It is, therefore, proper to conclude that personally interdicted individuals certainly must be considered not less worthy than *excommunicati vitandi.*

It has been considered necessary to consider Matrimony apart from the other Sacraments, because in many respects it widely differs from them.

Inasmuch as Matrimony is one of the seven Sacraments, one under the ban of personal interdict is forbidden to receive it.[101] Therefore, if, despite this prohibitive law, one, nevertheless, receives the Sacrament of Matrimony, without doubt, he commits a serious sin.

It will be remembered that the ministers of the Sacrament of Matrimony are the contracting parties themselves. Hence, there is a double prohibition against a personally interdicted individual to contract marriage, because such persons are forbidden both to administer and to receive the Sacraments.[102] It is certain that the contracting parties are bound *sub gravi* to be in the state of grace, inasmuch as

[99] Can. 1152.

[100] Vermeersch-Creusen, *Epitome*, II, n. 469.

[101] Can. 2275, n. 2; Can. 2260, §1.

[102] Can. 2275, n. 2.

they are the recipients of the Sacrament. It is probable that the contracting parties do not sin gravely by administering the Sacrament of Matrimony while in mortal sin. This opinion is based on the fact that the contracting parties are not *ordained* for the administration of the Sacrament. In this connection, Genicot-Salsmans remarks: "...a gravi peccato excusantur: Laici...qui comparti *matrimonium* administrant (quamquam hi graviter peccant quatenus idem sacramentum in hoc malo statu suscipiunt.)" [103]

According to the legislation of the Code,[104] a pastor is forbidden to assist at the marriage of one who is a public sinner, or who is notoriously under the ban of censure, if such a person refuses to make a good confession or to be reconciled to the Church, unless a grave and urgent cause is present, concerning which the pastor should consult the Ordinary if it be possible to do so. Thus, it can be seen that a notoriously interdicted individual is forbidden to contract marriage by virtue of Canon 1066.

The censure of personal interdict may be notorious either by reason of fact or by reason of law. Thus, the censure is notorious by notoriety of fact when the delinquent has committed a delict, which is publicly known to be punished by a censure, and which cannot be concealed by any tergiversation, or excused by any support of law. A censure is notorious by notoriety of law after a declaratory or condemnatory sentence has been passed, or after a judicial confession of the delinquent according to the provision of Canon 1750.[105]

If a notoriously interdicted person wishes to contract marriage, before doing so he must be reconciled to the Church by obtaining absolution from his censure. Since a censure concerns the external forum, it should be absolved in the same forum. It is provided in Canon 2251 that if absolution from a censure is given in the internal forum, it affects both fora. If, however, absolution from a cen-

---

[103] *Institutiones Theologiae Moralis*, 10 ed., II, n. 115.

[104] Can. 1066.

[105] Canon 2197.

sure is given in the internal forum, the person absolved may, if there is no danger of scandal, act as if he were absolved in the external forum also. However, if the absolution is neither proven nor can be legitimately presumed in the external forum, the competent Superior can enforce the observance of the censure in the external forum until absolution is obtained in that forum also. According to Vermeersch-Creusen,[106] the Superior not only is permitted, but should enforce the censure in the external forum if legitimate satisfaction which is morally possible has not yet been made. Sole remarks: "Sed notetur quod Superior nihili facere debet absolutionem concessam tantum in foro interno, si absolutus non dedit debitam satisfactionem partis laesae, et haec instet ut sibi detur congrua satisfactio." [107] It remains to be said, however, that in cases in which absolution from a censure in the internal forum can be lawfully presumed, the Superior may accept this absolution as sufficient for the external forum.[108]

Unless a notoriously interdicted individual who desires to contract marriage is first absolved from his censure, the pastor may not assist at the marriage, save in very grave cases, and even in these cases the pastor should consult the Ordinary.

Thus far, the Sacrament of Matrimony has been considered from the point of view of the recipient; in other words, whether or not it may be received by notoriously interdicted individuals. Now, another phase is to be considered, namely, the assistance at marriages by notoriously interdicted priests.

Concerning the valid assistance of pastors and local Ordinaries at marriages, the Code [109] provides that they can validly assist at marriages from the day on which they take canonical possession of their respective parishes or dioceses *unless through a sentence they have been excommunicated,*

---

[106] *Epitome*, III, n. 450.

[107] *De Delictis et Poenis*, n. 185.

[108] Cappello, *De Censuris*, n. 98; Sole, *ibidem*.

[109] Can. 1095, §1, n. 1.

interdicted or suspended from office or have been declared as such.

From the beginning, it must be kept in mind that the right or power by virtue of which pastors assist at marriages, is not jurisdiction. There is, however, a great similarity between this right and jurisdiction itself. Like jurisdiction, the right to assist at marriages is obtained by virtue of an office and can be delegated to others.[110] Likewise, as acts of jurisdiction cannot be validly placed by one against whom a declaratory or condemnatory sentence has been passed, so a pastor or local Ordinary against whom a declaratory or condemnatory sentence of interdict has been passed cannot validly assist at marriages.[111]

It is to be noted that this right to assist at marriages is lost only by interdicted pastors or Ordinaries after a declaratory or condemnatory sentence has been passed. Therefore, if a pastor or Ordinary simply incurs a censure of personal interdict, they may continue to assist validly at marriages in their respective territories, provided, of course, all other requirements are satisfied. A question will naturally arise as to whether such a pastor could licitly assist at marriages. Although a priest assisting at marriages does not administer a Sacrament, nevertheless, his assistance would be illicit by reason of the Sacramentals which are joined to the assistance at marriage.[112]

As jurisdiction may be delegated to others, so, too, the right to assist at marriages may be delegated to others by pastors and local Ordinaries.[113] It is important to note that the Code says: *Parochus et loci Ordinarius, qui matrimonio possunt valide assistere, possunt quoque alii sacerdoti licentiam dare ut intra fines sui territorii matrimonio valide assistat.* From this, it is clear that after a declaratory or condemnatory sentence has been passed against a pastor or Ordinary, he not only loses his own right to assist validly at marriages, but because of the very reason that

---

[110] Hyland, *Excommunication*, p. 103.

[111] Can. 1095, §1, n. 1.

[112] Can. 2261, §1.

[113] Can. 1095, §2.

he cannot validly assist, he cannot delegate others to assist.[114] Likewise, concerning this matter Vlaming writes: "Pro valida concessione requiritur: (1) ut momento quo delegans licentiam concedit ipse valide assistere *iam* possit et *adhuc possit.*" [115] In like manner, Cappello writes: "Quare delegare possunt omnes et *soli* qui iure ordinario valide matrimonio assistunt, scil. parochus et loci Ordinarius, et quidem prout ipsimet ratione officii ac territorii valide assistere possunt." [116]

Here some consideration must be given to the legislation of Canon 1044. Inasmuch as even *post sententiam* interdicted priests may hear the confession of any of the faithful in danger of death,[117] it seems that they may also validly use the faculty granted in Canon 1044. In the first place, one must arrive at some understanding of Canon 1043 of which Canon 1044 is complementary. Thus, it is provided in Canon 1043 that in urgent danger of death, for the sake of quieting the conscience, or, if the case requires, to legitimatize the children, local Ordinaries are authorized to dispense from the form to be observed for the celebration of marriage; they (the Ordinaries) may also dispense from all impediments of ecclesiastical law, whether these impediments be public or occult, even if they be multiple, excepting the impediment arising from the Sacred Order of Priesthood, and from the impediment of affinity in the direct line, when the marriage has been consummated; the local Ordinaries may dispense their subjects wheresoever they may happen to be, and also all (who are not their subjects) who are actually in the territories of the Ordinaries; care must be taken to avoid scandal, and if a dispensation is given from disparity of worship or of mixed religion, the usual promises should be made. Canon 1044 extends the faculty granted by Canon 1043. Thus under the same conditions as have been mentioned in Canon 1043, and when the Ordinary cannot be reached, the faculty

[114] Knecht, *Handbuch des Katholischen Eherechts*, p. 128; Hilling, *Das Eherecht des Codex Juris Canonici*, §34 (pp. 101-105).

[115] *Praelectiones Juris Matrimonii*, n. 572.

[116] *De Sacramentis*, III, n. 673.

[117] Can. 2261, §3.

granted to Ordinaries is extended to the pastor, to the priest assisting at marriage according to the provision of Canon 1098, n. 2, and also to the confessor; the confessor, however, may use this faculty only in the internal forum and in the act of sacramental confession.

Canon 1098 provides that in case the proper pastor or the Ordinary, or a priest delegated by either of them, cannot be reached without grave inconvenience, Matrimony may be celebrated both validly and licitly before the witnesses alone, if one of the parties is in danger of death, also when it is prudently foreseen that the impossibility to reach a competent minister will last for a month. It is further provided that in either of the cases just mentioned, if a priest is nearby who can be present, he should be called, and should assist at the marriage together with the witnesses, with the provision, however, that the marriage is valid before the witnesses alone.[118]

From the wording of the Canon, the obligation seems to include the calling of any priest, even if he be under censure. For, Canon 1098, n. 2, states: "*In utroque casu, si praesto sit alius sacerdos qui adesse possit, vocari et, una cum testibus matrimonio assistere debet.*" It will, therefore, be noted that these words are quite universal in their content; they make no modifications or reservations. Concerning this matter, Augustine writes: "The priest may be any priest, even one under censure, or of some other diocese, because 'qui adesse possit' must, we believe, be taken in the sense of physical, not moral possibility." [119] Likewise, Petrovits [120] concludes that the words *alius sacerdos* allow the inference that the parties must request the presence of any priest even if he be under excommunication.

There seems, however, to be little necessity for controversy in this matter because, under the circumstances related in Canon 1098, the obligation of calling any priest (even one in good standing) is but a slight one. Thus,

---

118 Can. 1098, n. 2.

119 *Commentary*, V, 295.

120 *The New Church Law on Matrimony*, n. 501.

Vermeersch-Creusen remark: "Obligatio vocandi sacerdotem vere imponitur, sed non sub gravi ex solo praecepto; aliter, dixeris, si dubia sint de impedimento, vel ex praesentia sacerdotis facile obtenta gravia quaedam mala vitari possint." [121] The same authors, however, hold that a priest should be called, even if he be under censure, without the exception, however, of a *vitandus*.[122]

It remains to be said, therefore, that in cases in which no priest is available but a *post sententiam* interdicted priest, *per se* the contracting parties are not bound to call him; at least, they would not be bound under grave obligation.

Of course, it will be admitted by all that when there is danger of death, such a priest should not only assist at the marriage, but he may also administer Sacraments and Sacramentals according to the provisions of Canon 2261, §3. But may such a priest assist at a marriage in the other extraordinary state of affairs mentioned in Canon 1098? In other words, when it is prudently foreseen that the inability on the part of the contracting parties to reach the pastor or the Ordinary, or a priest delegated by either of them, will continue for a month, may a *post sententiam* interdicted priest assist at the marriage? Since the Code makes no explicit exception, it would seem that he can. For, Canon 1098, n. 2, states: "*Si praesto sit alius sacerdos*..." From this phrase, it is difficult to understand how any author would deny that a *post sententiam* interdicted priest may assist at marriage according to the provisions of Canon 1098. On the other hand, it is to be admitted that the active or passive assistance of a censured priest at any divine function is, at most, only tolerated by the Church. Thus, even in danger of death, a notoriously excommunicated or interdicted priest may administer other Sacraments and Sacramentals (besides Penance) only when asked by the dying person to do so, and even then when no other priests are present.[123] Therefore, since the presence

[121] *Epitome*, II, n. 406.

[122] *Ibidem*.

[123] Can. 2261, §3.

of another priest, as stipulated in Canon 1098, n. 2, is not required for the validity, it would seem to be more in conformity with the mind of the Church not to call for a priest who is interdicted by sentence. Moreover, the Church merely tolerates a *post sententiam* censured priest to assist actively or passively at divine offices only when there is question of avoiding greater evils, for example, to prevent one of the faithful from dying without the consolation of the Sacraments.

It seems that any priest who assists at a marriage according to the provision of Canon 1098, n. 2, may also make use of the power of dispensing mentioned in Canon 1044, only under the circumstances, however, mentioned in Canons 1043 and 1044. Thus, when one of the parties is in danger of death, and the Ordinary cannot be reached, then for the purpose of quieting the conscience, or if the case demands it, to legitimatize the children, a priest who assists at marriage in virtue of Canon 1098, n. 2, may dispense from the form prescribed for the celebration of Matrimony, together with all impediments arising from ecclesiastical law, whether such impediments be public or occult, except the impediment arising from the Sacred Order of Priesthood, and the impediment arising from affinity in the direct line when the marriage has been consummated. Therefore, it seems that a priest assisting at marriage by virtue of Canon 1098, n. 2, even if he be interdicted by a condemnatory sentence or has been declared as such, may make use of the faculty granted in Canon 1044. It must be remembered that, although his presence is not required for the validity of the marriage in such circumstances as are related in Canon 1098, nevertheless, there may be diriment impediments which would render the marriage invalid; therefore, a priest who assists at such a marriage in virtue of Canon 1098, even though he be notoriously interdicted, certainly should be called to dispense from the impediments.[124]

---

[124] Can. 1044, Can. 1045.

IV.—Rights Denied Interdicted Persons According to Canon 2265

According to Canon 2275, n. 3, those under personal interdict are held to the provisions of Canon 2265, in the same manner as excommunicated persons.

Canon 2265.—§1. Quilibet excommunicatus:

n. 1. Prohibetur iure eligendi, praesentandi, nominandi;

n. 2. Nequit consequi dignitates, officia, beneficia, pensiones ecclesiasticas aliudve munus in Ecclesia;

n. 3. Promoveri nequit ad ordines;

§2. Actus tamen positus contra praescriptum §1, nn. 1, 2, non est nullus, nisi positus fuerit ab excommunicato vitando vel ab alio excommunicato post sententiam declaratoriam vel condemnatoriam; quod si haec sententia lata fuerit, excommunicatus nequit praeterea gratiam ullam pontificiam valide consequi, nisi in pontificio rescripto mentio de excommunicatione fiat.

A.—The Rights of Electing, Presenting and Nominating

According to Canon 2265, §1, n. 1, an excommunicated person is forbidden to exercise the right of election, presentation and nomination. Now, this same discipline is to be applied also to those under the ban of personal interdict.[125] As is evident, there is question here of ecclesiastical offices. According to the Code,[126] an ecclesiastical office in a broad sense, is any duty which is legitimately performed for a spiritual end. In the strict sense, however, it is a position permanently established by divine or ecclesiastical authority, and to be conferred according to the discipline of Canon Law; moreover, an ecclesiastical office in the strict sense necessarily has connected with it some participation in the ecclesiastical power of Orders or Jurisdiction. In law, the term *ecclesiastical office* is to be taken in the strict sense unless the contrary is evident from the context itself. According to Vermeersch-Creusen, an ecclesiastical office is understood in the strict sense when it is distinguished by

[125] Can. 2275, n. 3.
[126] Can. 145.

the following circumstances: "Est *munus sacrum*, tum quia finem supernaturalem respicit, tum quia sive a Christo sive ab Ecclesia est statutum; stabile est, stabilitate sc. *objectiva*, ita ut ex institutione Christi aut jure ecclesiastico constituatur in Ecclesia modo perpetuo certum potestatis spiritualis gradus, certus jurium spiritualium complexus clerico conferendus aut semper aut quotiens adjuncta jure definita recurrunt, puta munus episcopi, vicarii capitularis, administratoris diocesis, etc.; ejus *collatio* certis juris *communis* regulis determinatur, etiamsi beneficentia privatae personae erigi, potuit, neque a beneplacito Superioris omnino pendet; annexam habet aliquam saltem *potestatem*, sive ordinis sive jurisdictionis." [127]

Without canonical provision, one cannot validly obtain an ecclesiastical office.[128] By canonical provision is understood the giving of the ecclesiastical office by competent ecclesiastical authority and in accordance with the regulations of the Code.[129] This provision or appointment to an ecclesiastical office is done: (1) by the free appointment by a legitimate Superior; (2) by institution when presentation by a patron or nomination has preceded; (3) by confirmation or admission, if election or postulation has preceded; (4) by simple election, and the acceptance on the part of the one elected, if the election itself does not need confirmation.[130] "Verba *provisio, collatio* et *institutio* in veteri jure tamquam synonima non raro adhibebantur ad designandam concessionem officii in genere. In Codice, collati, conferre de libera collatione per oppositionem ad necessariam collationem seu institutionem adhibentur." [131]

Election in a broad sense signifies any legitimate designation of a person to an office.[132] In a strict canonical sense, *election* signifies the calling of a person to an ecclesiastical office by those who have the right of suffrage.[133]

---

[127] *Epitome*, I, n. 227.
[128] Can. 147, §1.
[129] Can. 147, §2.
[130] Can. 148, §1.
[131] Vermeersch-Creusen, *Epitome*, I, n. 231.
[132] Vermeersch-Creusen, *ibidem.*
[133] Cappello, *De Censuris*, n. 153.

Presentation is the right of designating a cleric to a vacant office by a competent Superior. The Code, in relating the privileges of patrons, mentions the privilege of presenting a cleric for a vacant parish or vacant benefice.[134] It seems that the right of presentation is usually identified with the *jus patronatus.* Likewise, Canon 1464, speaking of presentation, states: "Praesentatio fieri debet loci Ordinario, cujus est judicare utrum idonea sit persona praesentata."

The term nomination is often employed in a very general sense to signify any kind of provision for an ecclesiastical office.[135] Nomination, as distinguished from presentation and election, is the designation of a cleric who has fitness for a vacant office, which choice is accepted by the Bishop or other competent Superior. The right of nomination depends upon an Apostolic privilege and not upon the *jus patronatus.*[136] In the strict meaning of the term, it denotes the naming of a person for an ecclesiastical office which precedes the formal designation to the Superior.[137]

According to the present discipline of the Code, those under excommunication are forbidden to use the right of election, presentation and nomination.[138] This same discipline must also be applied to those under personal interdict.[139] This same disposition of law existed before the Code. Thus Schmalzgrueber wrote: "Per excommunicationem, excommunicatus fit incapax consequendi aliquod beneficium ecclesiasticum, et consequenter, electio, praesentatio, nominatio, quo excommunicatus ad beneficium tale promovetur, omnino nulla, et irrita est." [140] It will be noticed that this provision of the law includes not only notoriously interdicted individuals, or those against whom a declaratory or condemnatory sentence has been passed, but also anyone who is under a personal interdict. It is to be

---

134 Can. 1455, n. 1.

135 Hyland, *Excommunication,* p. 152.

136 Schmalzgrueber, lib. I, tit. VI, n. 2.

137 Wernz, *Jus Decretalium*, II, n. 352.

138 Can. 2265, §1, n. 1.

139 Can. 2275, n. 3.

140 Pars IV, tit. XXXIX, n. 147.

noted, however, that the exercise of the right of electing, presenting or nomination in defiance to the prohibition of Canon 2265, §1, n. 1, is not necessarily invalid. The Canon uses the words: "Prohibetur iure, eligendi, praesentandi, nominandi." Therefore, if one under personal interdict, nevertheless, makes use of the right of election, although he acts unlawfully, his vote is not invalid unless a declaratory or condemnatory sentence has been passed against him.[141] Concerning this point, Vermeersch-Creusen write: "Omnis isti actus *valide*, etsi illicite, ponuntur, dummodo excommunicatio jure notoria ne sit vel excommunicatus ne sit vitandus." [142] Although the above quotation of Vermeersch-Creusen refers explicitly only to those under excommunication, nevertheless those under personal interdict are included in this provision of the law.[143] Those who are interdicted by a sententence are incapable of electing (voting).[144] Therefore, if such a person casts a vote at an election for an ecclesiastical office, his vote is absolutely invalid. Such a vote, however, does not necessarily render the entire proceeding or the election invalid. Hence, according to Canon 167, §2, the election is valid, unless it is known that the invalid vote was such as to sway or decide the election; in other words, when it is known that the one elected would not have had the number of votes required for election without the vote of the notoriously censured person.

With regard to the right of postulation, Haas [145] holds that it is denied only in cases of juristic persons, e.g., chapters.

B.—Acquisition of Dignities, Offices, Benefices, Etc.

Canon 2265, §1, n. 2, states that an excommunicated person cannot acquire dignities, offices, benefices, ecclesiastical pensions or any other position in the Church. This

---

[141] Can. 2275, n. 3; Can. 2265, §2.
[142] *Epitome*, III, n. 467.
[143] Can. 2275, n. 3.
[144] Can. 167, §1, n. 3.
[145] *Das Interdikt*, p. 110, §5.

legislation applies also to those under personal interdict.[145a]

A *dignity* is generally a benefice to which is attached some jurisdiction, or at least some pre-eminence together with certain honorary prerogatives. According to the present discipline, dignities generally do not embrace jurisdiction.[146]

An *ecclesiastical office,* in a broad sense, is any duty which is legitimately exercised towards a spiritual end. In the strict sense of the term, an *ecclesiastical office* is a position permanently instituted by divine or ecclesiastical authority, which position is to be conferred according to the regulations of the Code, and entails some participation in the ecclesiastical power of Orders or Jurisdiction.[147]

An *ecclesiastical benefice* is a juridical entity permanently established by ecclesiastical authority, consisting of a sacred office together with the right of receiving the revenue which accrues from the endowment of the said office.[148]

According to Vermeersch-Creusen,[149] an *ecclesiastical pension* is "jus percipiendi partem fructuum alicujus beneficii vel mensae, titulo non perpetuo." Cappello[150] defines an ecclesiastical pension as follows: "*Pensio ecclesiastica* est portio aliqua fructuum beneficii legitime clerico concessa. Non est confundenda cum pensione *laicali,* quae independenter ab Ecclesia constituitur et fructus beneficii non afficit."

Aliudve munus denotes any other office or duty instituted and exercised towards a spiritual end.[151] From the definition it is evident that the term *aliudve munus* may be taken in a very broad sense.

According to the present discipline, excommunicated and interdicted persons[152] cannot acquire ecclesiastical dignities, offices, pensions or any other position in the Church.[153] If, however, despite the prohibition just mentioned, an in-

---

[145a] Can. 2275, n. 3.
[146] Cappello, *De Censuris,* n. 154.
[147] Can. 145, §1.
[148] Can. 1409.
[149] *Epitome,* I, 207.
[150] *De Censuris,* n. 154.
[151] Cappello, *ibidem.*
[152] Can. 2275, n. 3.
[153] Can. 2265, §1, n. 2.

terdicted person, nevertheless, were appointed to an office or benefice, and accepted it, his acquisition of the office or benefice would certainly be illicit but not invalid.[154] It seems, however, that the acquisition of an ecclesiastical office, benefice or pension would be invalid if conferred upon an interdicted person against whom a declaratory or condemnatory sentence had been passed.[155] Thus, it seems that the discipline set forth in the Code is so clear that there is little possibility of controversy. The general regulation prohibiting the acquisition of ecclesiastical offices and the like includes all those under personal interdict; consequently, if such a person is granted and accepts an office, benefice or pension, both the conferring and the accepting of it would be illicit but not necessarily invalid. However, if there is question of an interdicted individual against whom a declaratory or condemnatory sentence has been passed, the unlawful acquisition would be also invalid.[156]

What is to be said of interdicted persons who had acquired their offices or benefices before they became interdicted? Certainly, they do not forfeit their offices and benefices, because even those under excommunication who hold offices and benefices do not forfeit them.[157] For it is stated in the last-quoted Canon that after a declaratory or condemnatory sentence, an excommunicate is deprived of the fruits which arise from his office, benefice, pension or any position which he has in the Church. The Canon itself implies that the excommunicate still holds his office, etc., for it uses the clause, *si quod habet in Ecclesia.* Therefore, if excommunicates still retain offices and the like, after a condemnatory or declaratory sentence, certainly it cannot be urged that those under personal interdict forfeit them.

Are those under personal interdict deprived of the fruits which accrue from their offices, benefices, pensions and the like after a declaratory or condemnatory sentence has been

---

154 Haas, *Das Interdikt,* p. 110.

155 Can. 2265, §2; Can. 2275, n. 3.

156 Can. 2265, §2.

157 Can. 2266.

issued against them? It might be argued that since those under excommunication are deprived of them,[158] *a pari*, those under personal interdict are also deprived of them. But this argument is invalid, because Canon 2275, n. 3, states that those under personal interdict are held to the provisions of Canon 2265, but it does not state that they are held to the provisions of Canon 2266. What is contained in Canon 2266 applies only to those under excommunication, and is not to be extended to those under personal interdict since the Code itself makes no such extension. Nor can it be argued that the two cases are parallel, and that therefore the punishments should be equal; for Canon 20 expressly states that penalties are not to be extended to parallel cases. Therefore, in this matter a strict interpretation is to be followed. Consequently, if one possesses a certain ecclesiastical office or benefice, he continues to hold his office or benefice together with the fruits which arise therefrom, even if a declaratory or condemnatory sentence of personal interdict has been issued against him.

C.—Prohibition Against the Reception of Orders

Canon 2265, §1, n. 3, states that no excommunicated person may be elevated to Orders. This measure of discipline applies also to those under personal interdict.[159]

Although the ceremony of Tonsure is not a Sacrament and not even an order, nevertheless it must be considered as included here. In Canon Law, the terms *ordinare, ordo* and *ordinatio* embrace not only the episcopal consecration, the three major orders and the four minor orders, but also first tonsure, unless the contrary is obvious from the wording of the text.[160]

The provision of Canon 2265, §1, n. 3, whereby excommunicated persons may not be promoted to Orders, applies with equal force to those under personal interdict.[161] It is certain that the term *ordines* here includes not only epis-

[158] Can. 2266; cfr. Can. 2340.
[159] Can. 2275, n. 3.
[160] Can. 950.
[161] Can. 2275, n. 3.

copal consecration, the major orders and the minor orders, but even tonsure.[162] It will be noticed that the prohibition discussed in Canon 2265, §1, n. 3, is already contained, at least in part, in Canon 2260, §1, which states that excommunicates are forbidden to receive the Sacraments. Thus, orders are forbidden to excommunicated and interdicted persons only in so far as they are Sacraments according to the prohibition of Canon 2260, §1. Consequently, as far as Canon 2260, §1, obtains, only the reception of the episcopal consecration, priesthood and deaconship are forbidden. This same canon forbids the reception of Sacramentals by excommunicated or interdicted persons, only after a declaratory or condemnatory sentence has been issued against them. Canon 2265, §1, n. 3, however, is more general in its extent; for it forbids the reception of all orders without regard to the presence or absence of the sacramental character. The canon does not distinguish; it simply states: "*Promoveri nequit ad ordines.*" And in Canon Law, the term *ordines* includes even the minor orders and first tonsure.[163] Therefore, even the minor orders and first tonsure are included in the prohibition of Canon 2265, §1, n. 3.

Although n. 3 of Canon 2265, §1, which concerns the prohibition against receiving orders by excommunicated and interdicted persons, uses the term *nequit,* nevertheless there is evidently question here of licit and not valid reception of orders. Consequently, Canon 2265, §1, n. 3, states a grave prohibition and nothing more. Therefore, such prohibition in no wise renders the reception of orders invalid.

Haas [164] states that an interdicted person cannot receive orders validly, a statement which is difficult to reconcile with the principles of Theology. It is to be admitted that if the matter and form of the order are employed, and if the ordaining Bishop has the intention of doing what the Church does, and, finally, if the recipient (although under personal interdict) has the intention of receiving the order,

[162] Augustine, *Commentary,* VIII, 191.

[163] Can. 950.

[164] *Das Interdikt,* p. 111.

the reception is valid. With regard to the Episcopate and the major orders, it is to be remembered that their validity depends on what is required by divine law, and not upon the presence or absence of censures. With regard to the four minor orders and tonsure, it seems that their validity depends upon the requirements constituted by ecclesiastical law; the Church, however, has not ordained that freedom from censures is an essential condition for the valid reception of the Sacramentals. In connection with this point, Augustine writes: "A question might arise as to minor orders and tonsure, whether they would be invalidly conferred by a prelate who is under a declaratory sentence of excommunication, because these orders are not, properly speaking, Sacraments, but merely Sacramentals. Comparing Canon 2372 with our text, their validity can be solidly defended." [165]

Therefore, it must be concluded that the prohibition contained in Canon 2265, §1, n. 3, in no wise affects the validity of orders received by one who is under excommunication or personal interdict. It is certainly to be admitted that if one so censured received orders, he would be guilty of grave sin in showing open defiance to the mandates of the Church.

It must also be stated that the ordinary power of jurisdiction for the hearing of confessions ceases after a priest has a declaratory or condemnatory sentence of interdict passed against him.[166]

D.—Papal Rescripts

According to the provision of Canon 2265, §2, no one under excommunication against whom a declaratory or condemnatory sentence has been passed, can validly acquire any papal favor, unless mention of the censure of excommunication is made in the text of the papal rescript. This regulation applies also to those under personal inter-

---

[165] *Commentary*, VIII, 191.

[166] Can. 873, §3.

dict (if a declaratory or condemnatory sentence has been passed against them).[167]

In general, a rescript is an answer given in writing either by the Holy See or by an Ordinary to a person seeking a response to a question, or to one seeking a favor.[168]

Rescripts may be of two kinds: (1) rescripts of justice, which are responses containing a provision to a judicial controversy or to the administration of justice; (2) rescripts of grace which grant favors of some kind.[169] A rescript of grace may grant a privilege or dispensation.[170]

This inability on the part of *post sententiam* excommunicated or interdicted persons, has to do only with rescripts of favor.[171] In this point the Code differs from the old law which included even rescripts of justice in the regulation.[172] Moreover, all censured persons were considered as unworthy and ineligible to receive all papal favors.[173]

Whether or not privileges and dispensations are included in this inability on the part of *post sententiam* interdicted persons to acquire papal favors is not easy to decide. It would seem that privileges and dispensations are not included in this prohibition, because of the fact that Canon 36, §2, makes an explicit distinction between favors and dispensations. Likewise, Canon 62 distinguishes between a *simple favor* and a *privilege* or *dispensation.* On the other hand, it seems that this inability on the part of *post sententiam* interdicted persons affects also privileges and dispensations, because of the universal character of the words "gratiam ullam pontificiam" which occur in Canon 2265, §2. According to the common signification of the words "gratia ulla," all kinds of favors or privileges certainly should be included in this regulation. In this connection, Cappello [174] points out that privileges and dispensa-

---

[167] Can. 2275, n. 3.

[168] Vermeersch-Creusen, *Epitome,* I, n. 123.

[169] Hyland, *Excommunication,* p. 160.

[170] Can. 62.

[171] Cappello, *De Censuris,* n. 157.

[172] C. 26, X, *de rescriptis,* I, 3; C. I, *de rescriptis,* I, 3, in VI°.

[173] Sole, *De Delictis et Poenis,* n. 230.

[174] *De Censuris,* n. 157.

tions are here included, because the words *"ulla gratia"* are of such a generic character as to embrace favors of any kind, and, consequently, even privileges and dispensations are included in this regulation.

Thus, Cappello writes: "Incapacitas refertur ad gratias *pontificias* dumtaxat, seu concedendas a Sede Apostolica, hoc est sive immediate a R. Pontifice sive ab aliqua Sacra Conregatione aut Officio Romanae Curiae." [175] Thus, graces and favors granted to a *post sententiam* interdicted person by his Ordinary or by another Prelate would not be null and void by reason of Canon 2265, §2. Furthermore, there is question here only of new favors; in other words, the acquiring of a favor which one did not enjoy before the sentence was passed against him. Consequently, if one has acquired certain papal favors, and is later interdicted by a condemnatory sentence, or has been declared such by a declaratory sentence, he is in no wise to be deprived of these favors which were obtained before the passing of the declaratory or condemnatory sentence against him. The contrary, of course, would be true, if the rescript granting the papal favor so provided. In practice, however, a provision of this kind is never added to a rescript.[176]

Before the Constitution "Sapienti consilio" of September 29, 1908, all those under censure were held as unworthy of any pontifical favor, and any rescript asked and received by an excommunicated person, whether *toleratus* or *vitandus* was *ipso jure* invalid.[177] As is evident, an exception was admitted in cases which concerned a censure or an appeal from the sentence of a censure.[178] Thus, it was the practice of the Roman Curia, in granting rescripts, to give absolution *ad cautelam* from all censures.[179] The reason for granting absolution in this manner was to insure the validity of the rescript.

Pope Pius X, however, in the *Normae Peculiares*, which were jointly published with the Constitution *"Sapienti*

[175] *De Censuris*, n. 157.
[176] Cappello, *ibidem*.
[177] Sole, *De Delictis et Poenis*, n. 230.
[178] C. 1, *de rescriptis*, I, 3, in VI°.
[179] Wernz, I, n. 151.

consilio," decreed that from November 3, 1908, all favors and dispensations granted by the Holy See were genuine and legitimate, even when granted to those under censure, save in those cases in which a delinquent was nominally excommunicated, or when one was nominally suspended *a divinis.*[180]

This change effected by Pius X, with few changes, has been embodied into the Code, as can be seen from the provisions of Canons 2265, §2, 2275, n. 3, and 2283. Hence, unless the recipient is excommunicated, interdicted or suspended by legitimate ecclesiastical authority, and by means of a declaratory or condemnatory sentence, all rescripts granting papal favors are valid.

V.—Ecclesiastical Burial

Canon 2275, n. 4.—Carent sepultura ecclesiastica ad normam can. 1240, §1, n. 2.

Canon 1240.—§1, n. 2. Ecclesiastica sepultura privantur, nisi ante mortem aliqua dederint poenitentiae signa: Excommunicati vel interdicti post sententiam condemnatoriam vel declaratoriam.

The Code defines ecclesiastical burial as the transferring of the corpse to the church, and the conducting of funeral services over it, and interring it in a place lawfully reserved for the burial of the faithful departed.[181]

Who are entitled to ecclesiastical burial? According to Canon 1239, the reception of Baptism is the fundamental fact upon which the right to ecclesiastical burial is based. For it is therein stated that those who have not received Baptism are not to be admitted to ecclesiastical burial.

There is a provision, however, that catechumens, who, through no fault of their own, die without Baptism, are to be included among baptized persons, as far as ecclesiastical burial is concerned.[182] Finally, the general disposition of the law is that all baptized persons are to be given

180 *AAS*, I (1909), p. 64.

181 Can. 1204.

182 Can. 1239, §2.

ecclesiastical burial, unless they are expressly deprived of it by law.[183] Concerning the refusal on the part of the Church to grant ecclesiastical burial to the unworthy, Vermeersch-Creusen write: "Cum sepultura ecclesiastica ultimum sit communionis ecclesiasticae signum et pignus, neganda est *per se* omnibus qui in ecclesiam catholicam numquam ingressi sunt vel ab ea post baptismum publice defecerunt. Hoc supremo honore juste priventur etiam ii qui publicis iisque gravissimis delictis Ecclesiam quasi deseruerunt."[184]

Since the denial of ecclesiastical burial is a privation, the Canons treating of it must be interpreted strictly. Thus, for example, when there is doubt as to whether Baptism was conferred, or whether it was conferred validly, the deceased is to be given ecclesiastical burial according to the strict interpretation of the law.[185]

According to the discipline in force before the Code, those under personal interdict were to be denied ecclesiastical burial.[186] Accordingly, Schmalzgrueber writes: "Si interdictum sit personale, iterum constat sic interdictum privatum esse sepultura ecclesiastica, sive deinde generale illud sit, sive speciale." [187] This is also true of those who cause a local interdict to be imposed, because such persons really incurred a particular personal interdict.[188] Therefore if one under a personal interdict died without receiving absolution, or without showing some signs of repentence, he was to be buried outside consecrated ground. It was necessary, however, that the person be declared interdicted, because after the constitution *Ad evitanda,* no one was to be denied ecclesiastical burial by reason of censure, unless the person was first denounced by sentence.[189]

If it happened, contrary to the law forbidding ecclesiastical burial to those under personal interdict, that one so

---

183 Can. 1239, §3.

184 *Epitome,* II, n. 546.

185 Vermeersch-Creusen, *Epitome,* II, n. 547.

186 C. 8, *de priv.*, V, 8, in VI°.

187 Pars IV, tit. XXXIX, n. 377.

188 Schmalzgrueber, *ibidem.*

189 Schmalzgrueber, *ibidem.*

interdicted was buried in consecrated ground, it was not mandatory to exhume the body. The law concerning interdicted persons on this point differs from that concerning excommunicated persons. Thus, if the body of an excommunicated person were interred in consecrated ground, whether by error or contempt of the law, such a body was to be exhumed if it could be propertly discerned from the other bodies.[190]

It is stated in Canon 2275, n. 4 that those under personal interdict are deprived of ecclesiastical burial according to the provision of Canon 1240, §1, n. 2. It is therein stated that excommunicated and interdicted persons, provided a declaratory or condemnatory sentence has been issued against them, are to be deprived of ecclesiastical burial, unless, before their death, they showed some signs of repentance. Thus, a change in this point is introduced by the Code. Accordingly, Vermeersch-Creusen write: "Sub jure anteriore soli *excommunicati vitandi* sepultura ecclesiastica privabantur, vi principii 'quibus non communicavimus vivis, non communicemus defunctis.' "[191]

According to the present discipline, no one who showed signs of repentance before his death is to be denied ecclesiastical burial. Concerning those under personal interdict, the law provides that only those interdicted persons against whom a declaratory or a condemnatory sentence has been passed, are to be deprived of this last rite.[192] Hence, if one who under a personal interdict dies, he is not to be deprived of ecclesiastical burial by reason of his censure of interdict, so long as no sentence has been issued against him. In a case of this kind, however, circumstances might easily be such that the deceased would be deprived of ecclesiastical burial for some other reason. Thus, although no sentence has been issued against the interdicted person, he might be denied ecclesiastical burial because he was a notorious apostate, or because his death was caused from a duel, or because he was otherwise a notorious sinner.[193] It is always

190 Reiffenstuel, lib. V, tit. XXXIX, n. 215.

191 *Epitome,* II, n. 549.

192 Can. 1240, §1, n. 2.

193 Can. 1240, §1.

provided, however, that the deceased is never to be deprived of this last honor which the Church bestows upon her children, if, before his death, he showed some sign, however remote, of repentance.

Sufficient signs of repentance would be the asking for a priest for the purpose of confessing; begging God to pardon one's sins; invoking the names of God, the Blessed Virgin or the Saints, or the kissing of a crucifix or some other sacred object.[194] The testimony of one witness who saw or heard any of these signs, is sufficient for granting ecclesiastical burial to any censured person.[195]

It may be argued that scandal might arise by granting ecclesiastical burial to notoriously censured persons, or other public sinners, when it is not generally known that they did penance before death. In such cases, the scandal can be removed by a prudent revelation that penance was done in private. Hence, Vermeersch-Creusen write: "Ubi tamen scandalum paenitentia publica non est reparatum, istud revelatione paenitentiae privatae prudenter est tollendum." [196]

If in a particular case, there should be a positive doubt as to whether the interdicted person should receive ecclesiastical burial, the Ordinary should be consulted if there be sufficient time. If the doubt remains, the departed person should be given ecclesiastical burial; this is to be done, however, in such a manner that there is no danger of scandal.[197]

It is provided in Canon Law that those who are denied ecclesiastical burial, are also to be denied a funeral Mass, an anniversary Mass and any other public funeral service.[198] "Proinde vetita habenda est etiam Missa in die tertia, septima et trigesima." [199]

The *Missa exsequialis* is one which is celebrated with the body of the deceased in the church.[200] This expression

---

[194] Cappello, *De Censuris*, n. 158.
[195] Genicot-Salsmans, *Institutiones Theologiae Moralis*, II, n. 628.
[196] *Epitome*, II, n. 548.
[197] Can. 1240, §2.
[198] Can. 1241.
[199] Cappello, *De Censuris*, n. 158.
[200] Hyland, *Excommunication*, p. 86.

Missa exsequialis, however, is not to be considered as including ordinary *requiem Masses.*[201] Hence, Canon 1241 does not forbid the celebration of Mass, even of a *requiem Mass,* for such interdicted persons as have been denied ecclesiastical burial. Of course, this means that the Mass for the one who is denied ecclesiastical burial, must be altogether private and with all danger of scandal removed.[202]

It is always to be borne in mind that, aside from scandal or contempt, an ecclesiastical law does not bind under grave inconvenience, and, consequently, when very grave evils are likely to follow when ecclesiastical burial is denied, it may be granted in part or even in full; in a concession of this kind, however, great care must be taken to avoid scandal.[203]

If the body of a *post sententiam* interdicted person is buried in consecrated ground contrary to the provisions of Canon Law, it need not be exhumed. This is deduced from Canon 1242 which provides that the body of an *excommunicatus vitandus* is to be exhumed from the consecrated ground, if this can be done without a grave inconvenience, and buried in unblessed ground.[204] Since mention is made only of *excommunicati vitandi* in Canon 1242, it is to be concluded that the body of an interdicted person, even if a declaratory or condemnatory sentence has been passed against him, need not be exhumed.

The law depriving ecclesiastical burial is sanctioned by very severe penalties. Thus, those who dare to demand or force ecclesiastical burial to be given to those to whom it is denied by virtue of Canon 1240, §1, nn. 1 and 2, incur excommunication *latae sententiae;* furthermore, those who deliberately grant ecclesiastical burial to them incur an interdict *ab ingressu ecclesiae* reserved to the Ordinary.[205] This last-mentioned penalty can be incurred only by clerics, because only they can officially grant ecclesiastical burial.[206]

---

201 Quigley, *Condemned Societies,* p. 81.
202 Cappello, *De Censuris,* n. 158.
203 Vermeersch-Creusen, *Epitome,* II, n. 550.
204 Can. 1212.
205 Can. 2339.
206 Sole, *De Delictis et Poenis,* n. 367.

CHAPTER VI

Concessions in Favor of Those Personally Innocent

***Canon 2276.*—Qui interdicto locali vel interdicto in communitatem seu collegium subest, quin eidem causam dederit, nec alia censura prohibeatur, potest, si sit rite dispositus, Sacramenta recipere, ad normam canonum praecedentium, sine absolutione ab interdicto aliave satisfactione.**

Canon 2276 states that those who are under a local interdict or an interdict which is imposed upon a community or a corporation, but who have not been the cause of the interdict, and who are not otherwise censured, may receive the Sacraments according to the provision of the preceding Canons, provided, of course, that such persons be properly disposed; moreover, the Canon further states that, under the foregoing circumstances, there is no need for absolution from the interdict or any other satisfaction.

It is evident from the wording of this canon that the Church has made a laudable provision in favor of those who in no wise caused a local or general personal interdict. It can be readily seen from this enactment that it is the mind of the Church to lessen the hardships of the innocent as much as possible, when she finds it necessary to impose a local interdict or a personal interdict upon an entire community or moral body. Accordingly, the Church allows the innocent, even without receiving absolution or any other satisfaction, to receive the Sacraments according to the provisions laid down in the preceding canons.

It will be remembered that a local interdict is one which directly affects a place and only indirectly affects the persons living in the place; a personal interdict, on the other hand, is one which directly affects a person by depriving him of the use of certain sacred things.[1] Since Canon 2276 makes no distinction between general local and particular local interdicts, it is evident that those in whose favor this concession is made, may avail themselves of this privilege during any local interdict, whether it be general or particular.

The Code provides that those innocent of causing an interdict to be imposed are free to receive the Sacraments *in accordance with the provisions of the preceding canons.* The reason for such provision is because they are not free to receive Sacraments in a church which has been closed by reason of an interdict; consequently, they may receive Sacraments only in those churches in which services are allowed.[2]

Canon 2276 permits the innocent to receive the Sacraments, but this concession cannot be made to include the reception of Sacramentals. It is pointed out in Canon 19 that laws which contain an exception from another law must be interpreted strictly. Therefore only the reception of the Sacraments is permitted by virtue of Canon 2276.[3]

From the fact that those personally innocent of causing an interdict to be imposed are free to receive Sacraments *sine absolutione ab interdicto aliave satisfactione,* it can be deduced that local interdicts, whether general or particular, and personal interdicts which are imposed upon a community as such, are not, properly and strictly speaking, censures. This statement is confirmed and supported by Canon 2248, §1, which states that any censure, once contracted, is removed only by legitimate absolution. Therefore, the fact that the innocent are permitted to receive the Sacraments without any absolution from the interdict or any other satisfaction, certainly demonstrates that the interdicts in such circumstances as are here considered do not possess the real and essential character of censures.[4] It is also probable that all local interdicts and general personal interdicts, in so far as they affect the innocent, are

[1] Can. 2268, §2.

[2] Canons 2270-2272.

[3] Haas, *Das Interdikt*, p. 113.

[4] Sole, *De Delictis et Poenis*, n. 249.

not even penalties. Thus, Sole writes: "...imo, quoad insontes, ne poenae quidem sunt, quia ubi noxa non est, ibi nec poena esse potest, sed privationes quaedam, quibus amplius non tenetur, qui desinat esse illius corporis membrum." [5]

Moreover, it may be argued that the very nature of ecclesiastical penalties demonstrates that they are inflicted only upon offenders against the law, for the purpose of correcting them and vindicating ecclesiastical discipline. Thus, Canon 2215 states that an ecclesiastical penalty is the privation of a certain benefit, which is inflicted by legitimate authority upon the delinquent for the purpose of correcting him and in punishment of his delict. But in local interdicts and in interdicts imposed upon a community or college, there may be many persons in the place or in the community who in no manner whatever took part in the offense on account of which the interdict was imposed. It is for this reason, therefore, that the Church has provided in Canon 2276 that such persons should not suffer the privations entailed in the interdicts in so far as they individually are concerned.

Wherefore, both the determination of the Church to enforce her discipline, and her kindness and consideration towards her faithful children are at once apparent. It is a fact to be admitted by all that in every society there are some who are unfaithful to the principles and regulations of the society, and are, therefore, justly deprived of some or all of its benefits; the Church, although divinely established, is no exception. Therefore, if she is to discharge in a faithful manner the mission entrusted to her by Christ, she must punish her delinquent children. At the same time, however, the Church considers it not less important to extend every possible consideration and kindness towards her many loyal and faithful children. It is for this reason, therefore, and for this reason only, that the Church has established the legislation of Canon 2276.

---

[5] *Ibidem.*

CHAPTER VII

INTERDICTS FORBIDDING ENTRANCE INTO A CHURCH

Canon 2277.—Interdictum ab ingressu ecclesiae secumfert prohibitionem ne quis in ecclesia divina officia celebret vel eisdem assistat aut ecclesiasticam sepulturam habet; si autem assistat, non est necesse ut expellatur, nec, si sepeliatur, oportet ut cadaver amoveatur.

It is stated in Canon 2277 that an interdict *ab ingressu ecclesiae* entails the prohibition against celebrating divine offices in a church, or even to assist at them thereat; or to receive ecclesiastical burial; if, however, the person so interdicted nevertheless assists, it is not necessary to expel him, and if he has been given ecclesiastical burial, it is not necessary to exhume the body.

An interdict *ab ingressu ecclesiae* is a species of the particular personal interdict.[1] Cocchi calls it a milder form of the particular personal interdict.[2]

This type of interdict was quite common in the old law.[3] That this was a distinct species of interdict, is clear from the following: "Ut interdictum post se trahat hunc effectum, requiritur specialis sententia; quia non est annexus interdicto absolute, sed est quasi novum interdictum." [4]

According to the present disposition of the law, one who contracts an interdict *ab ingressu ecclesiae* is forbidden to assist actively or passively at divine offices in any church. He is likewise to be deprived of ecclesiastical burial. If,

[1] Sole, *De Delictis et Poenis*, n. 246; Chelodi, *Jus Poenale*, n. 41.

[2] *De Delictis et Poenis*, n. 96.

[3] "Is cui est ecclesiae interdictus ingressus (cum sibi per consequens censeatur in ipsa divinorum celebratio interdicta) irregularis efficitur, si contra interdictum hujusmodi divinis in ea se ingerat, in suo agens officio, sicut prius."—C. 20, *de sent. excom.*, V, 11, in VI°.

[4] Schmalzgrueber, Pars IV, tit. XXXIX, n. 379.

however, such a person assists at divine offices in disobedience of this canon, he need not be expelled, and if such a person is given ecclesiastical burial, it is not necessary to exhume the body.[5]

What is to be understood by the term *church?* "Ecclesiae nomine intelligitur aedes sacra divino cultui dedicata eum potissimum in finem ut omnibus Christifidelibus usui sit ad divinum cultum publice exercendum." [6] Hence, under the term *church,* public oratories, semi-public oratories and private oratories are not included.[7] According to the common concept, the term *church* is understood to include places set apart by the authority of the Bishop for the purpose of celebrating divine functions.[8]

One who is under an interdict *ab ingressu ecclesiae* is affected by it only when he is in a church properly so called. Hence, when outside a church, provided he has incurred no other censure, his status is the same as one not censured at all. Consequently, such a person may celebrate divine offices or assist at them in any oratory, whether public, semi-public or private. Hence, a priest interdicted *ab ingressu ecclesiae,* may even celebrate Mass in any oratory.[9] In this last respect, the present legislation differs from the opinion prevalent before the Code; for it was held that a priest interdicted *ab ingressu ecclesiae* could celebrate Mass and other divine offices in private oratories only. Thus, Schmalzgrueber wrote: "Privatus ergo ab ingressu ecclesiae non potest ordinem sacrum exercere in ecclesia, neque ibi officia divina audire; bene tamen hoc potest in oratorio privato, aut agro, nisi simul sit simpliciter interdictus quia non est privatio absoluta, sed limitata, scilicet in loco illo." [10] That a more liberal concession is granted by the present discipline is evident from the Code itself which clearly distinguishes between churches and oratories.[11]

---

[5] Can. 2277.
[6] Can. 1161.
[7] Cappello, *De Censuris,* n. 472.
[8] Schmalzgrueber, Pars IV, tit. XXXIX, n. 379; Cappello, *loc. cit.*
[9] Cappello, *De Censuris,* n. 472.
[10] Pars IV, tit. XXXIX, n. 379.
[11] Cfr. Canons 1161, 1188.

May a person who is interdicted *ab ingressu ecclesiae* receive Sacraments in a church? Upon this point, authors are not agreed. Woywod [12] maintains that the reception of the Sacraments is also forbidden to those under an interdict *ab ingressu ecclesiae.* He argues that the prohibition to celebrate divine offices and to assist at them includes both to the administration and to the reception of the Sacraments. The contrary opinion seems much more reasonable, because the Code makes no explicit prohibition against the reception of the Sacraments by those under an interdict *ab ingressu ecclesiae.*[13] It is also the opinion of Cappello [14] that persons under this type of interdict may receive the Sacraments in any church. This discussion is all the more practical since an interdict *ab ingressu ecclesiae* can be inflicted upon clerics and lay people alike.[15] The very wording of the Canon is so clear that there seems to be but little possibility for dispute. For Canon 2277 states that he who is bound by an interdict *ab ingressu ecclesiae* is deprived of the right of celebrating divine offices in a church, or assisting at them, and, finally, he is denied ecclesiastical burial. No other prohibition is laid down in the Canon; not one word is said about the reception of the Sacraments. Therefore, when the Code does not distinguish, there is no need for further distinction. Moreover, since there is question here of a penal character, the more favorable interpretation is to be followed.[16] Of course the prohibition against assisting at divine offices does not include assisting at the preaching of the word of God.[17] It might be argued that since assistance at divine services is forbidden to those under an interdict *ab ingressu ecclesiae, a fortiori* the reception of Sacraments is forbidden, because the reception of a Sacrament is more noble than mere assistance at divine offices. But such reasoning is juridically unsound; for, even if it be admitted that churches are established also

[12] *A Practical Commentary on Canon Law*, II, n. 219.
[13] Sole, *De Delictis et Poenis*, n. 247.
[14] *De Censuris*, n. 472.
[15] Augustine, *Commentary*, VIII, 215.
[16] Can. 2219, §1.
[17] Sole, *De Delictis et Poenis*, n. 247.

for the purpose of administering and receiving Sacraments, it cannot be concluded that by reason of a partial personal interdict that everything is forbidden to the person interdicted. On the contrary, only such things are forbidden as are expressly mentioned in the text of the law. Therefore, from the mere fact that the reception of a Sacrament is a more noble and more excellent benefit than the mere assistance at divine offices, it certainly does not follow that the reception of the Sacraments is *a fortiori* forbidden.[18] Therefore since there is no explicit prohibition in the text of the Canon to the contrary, it may be safely concluded that the reception of the Sacraments is permitted to those under an interdict *ab ingressu ecclesiae*.

It is also provided in Canon 2277 that those under this type of interdict are to be deprived of ecclesiastical burial, unless, of course, before their death, they showed some signs of repentance.[19]

What is to be understood by the term *ecclesiastica sepultura* in Canon 2277? Does this term include burial in any place legitimately set apart for the interment of the faithful,[20] or does it have reference only to burial in the church itself?[21] According to Augustine,[22] the prohibition denying ecclesiastical burial to those who contract an interdict of this kind, means that they must be buried outside of consecrated ground, without solemnity, and without the ecclesiastical rites which are performed in church. He further states that this prohibition concerning ecclesiastical burial has special reference to burial in the church itself; in other words the burial in the church of civil and ecclesiastical dignitaries.[23] That the prohibition against ecclesiastical burial contained in Canon 2277 has reference to

---

18 Schmalzgrueber, Pars IV, tit. XXXIX, n. 388.
19 Canon 1240.
20 Can. 1204.
21 Can. 1205, §2.
22 *Commentary*, VIII, 215.
23 Can. 1205, §2.

burial in the church only, is the opinion of Eichmann.[24] This opinion, however, is difficult to support. Probably the opinion is based on the fact that Canon 2277 deals specifically only with such functions as take place in the church. It might also be urged by the proponents of this opinion that the expression, "aut ecclesiasticam sepulturam habeat," in Canon 2277, must be understood to refer only to the phrase "in ecclesia," which occurs earlier in the same clause. But it must be noted that Canon 2277 contains two distinct prohibitions: the first prohibition concerns active and passive assistance at divine offices in a church; the second prohibition concerns ecclesiastical burial. Furthermore, when the Canon distinguishes between the celebration of divine offices and the assistance at divine offices, the particle "vel" is used; but when a distinction is drawn between the assistance (active or passive) at divine offices in a church and ecclesiastical burial, the particle "aut" is employed. Why the difference? Evidently different particles are here employed because Canon 2277 contains two distinct prohibitions. If this be so, the expression *aut ecclesiasticam sepulturam habeat* is not to be understood to extend only to such burials as take place *in ecclesia.* The prohibition against ecclesiastical burial, since it is distinct from the prohibition which precedes it in Canon 2277, should be understood in accordance with Canon 1204 which defines ecclesiastical burial as the translation of the body to the church, the celebration of funeral services over it in the church, and the depositing of it in a place legitimately set apart for the burial of the faithful departed. Therefore, if the prohibition against ecclesiastical burial contained in Canon 2277 is to be understood in the sense of the Code itself, the burial of those who contract an interdict *ab ingressu ecclesiae* can take place *neither in a church nor in a consecrated cemetery.* This is also the conclusion of Sole, who writes: "At sepultura ecclesiastica, tum in

---

[24] *Theologische Revue,* XXVIII (1929), 321. This author in a review of Haas, *Das Interdikt,* maintains that Canon 2277 forbids ecclesiastical burial to those who incur an interdict *ab ingressu ecclesiae,* only if the burial is to take place in the church.

ecclesia, tum in coemeterio benedicto, prohibetur nisi ante mortem aliqua dederit poenitentiae signa." [25]

When one is denied ecclesiastical burial, he is also deprived of a funeral Mass (Missa exsequialis), also an anniversary Mass or any other public funeral service.[26]

If, contrary to the prohibition against ecclesiastical burial one under an interdict *ab ingressu ecclesiae* is buried in a church or in a cemetery, his body need not be exhumed, whether such burial took place by ignorance, fraud or violence.[27]

Canon Law prescribes a penalty against those who violate an interdict *ab ingressu ecclesiae.* Thus, clerics in sacred orders and bound by an interdict of this kind, who, nevertheless, exercise an act of sacred orders in a church, become irregular *ex delicto.*[28]

An interdict *ab ingressu ecclesiae* may be inflicted both as a censure and as a vindictive penalty. Thus, if it is inflicted "in perpetuum vel ad tempus praefinitum vel ad beneplacitum Superioris," it is a vindictive penalty.[29] In all other cases it is a censure; likewise, when there is doubt, the presumption is that it is a censure.[30]

---

[25] *De Delictis et Poenis,* n. 247.
[26] Can. 1241.
[27] Augustine, *Commentary,* VIII, 215.
[28] Can. 985, n. 7.
[29] Can. 2291, n. 2.
[30] Can. 2255, §2.

CHAPTER VIII

INTERDICTS CONSTITUTED BY LAW

Before the Constitution "Apostolicae Sedis" of Pope Pius IX, there were many interdicts constituted by law.[1] According to Ferraris,[2] there were twenty-eight such interdicts; of this number, five were general local interdicts, three were particular local interdicts, six were general personal interdicts, and fourteen were particular personal interdicts. In his above-mentioned Constitution, Pope Pius IX abolished all of these interdicts with the exception of four. Consideration will be given to each of these interdicts during the discussion of the following canons.

I.—Penalty for Appealing from a Law of the Pope

Pope Pius IX, in the Constitution "Apostolicae Sedis"[3] decreed that bodies such as Universities, Colleges and Chapters which appeal to a future general council from the ordinances or decrees of the Pope, *ipso jure,* incur an interdict *speciali modo* reserved to the Holy Father. This provision of the Constitution "Apostolicae Sedis" has been incorporated bodily into the Code with the addition of the phrase *aliaeve personae morales.*[4] This expression appears to have a wider extension than the wording of the Constitution in question. Hence, such Corporations as Universities, Colleges, Chapters or any other moral person, no matter how named, incur this penalty if such a body appeals to a general council against the laws, ordinances or decrees of the reigning Pon-

[1] Crnica, *Modificationes in Tract. de Censuris,* p. 171.

[2] *Bibliotheca,* art. "Interdictum," Articula II-V.

[3] Cons. "Apostolicae Sedis" Oct. 12, 1869, VI, n. 1 (*Fontes,* n. 552).

[4] Can. 2332.

tiff. Therefore, according to Augustine,[5] a congress, senate or parliament could incur this penalty.

Since there is question here of penalties, there must be a strict interpretation. Consequently, the appeal must be made from the laws, decrees or ordinances issued by the Pope as such; that is, the laws, decrees or ordinances must emanate from the Roman Pontiff as the Supreme Ruler of the Church, and not as a temporal ruler, nor as an international judge.[6] In this connection, there is no question of decisions or ordinances issued by the Sacred Congregations and Tribunals.

It is to be noted that the *individual members* of the moral body do not incur this censure, but only the moral body as such. Concerning this point, Cappello writes: "Interdictum non fertur in *omnes* et *singulos*, sed in *communitatem*, uti talem. Proinde est interdictum personale *generale*, non vero *speciale*, cum corpora moralia afficiat, non autem singulares personas.[7] Nevertheless, each member of the moral body is bound by the interdict, even though he in no way caused it.[8]

There seems to be some doubt as to the meaning of the phrase *pro tempore existentis* in Canon 2332. Vermeersch-Creusen [9] maintain that this interdict is incurred only when an appeal is made from the laws, decrees or ordinances of the actually reigning Pope. This opinion is sharply questioned by Augustine,[10] who argues that such an interpretation nullifies the intention of the lawgiver; he further states that the laws, decrees and ordinances of the Pope are not intended only for his lifetime. Since the question at hand concerns a penal matter, it seems that the milder interpretation can safely be followed.[11] The opinion seems all the more tenable when it is fortified by that of Vermeersch-Creusen.

---

[5] *Commentary*, VIII, 328.
[6] *Augustine*, pp. 328, 329.
[7] *De Censuris*, n. 482.
[8] Cappello, *ibidem.*
[9] *Epitome*, III, n. 532.
[10] *Commentary*, VIII, 329.
[11] Can. 2219, §1.

Canon 2332 employs the expression "ad Universale Concilium appellantes," while the Constitution "Apostolicae Sedis" uses the expression "ad Universale Futurum Concilium appellantes." Before the Code, therefore, it could be argued that this interdict was not incurred by appealing to a present Universal Council.[12] The Code, however, omits the word *futurum,* and, consequently, according to the present discipline of Canon Law, the censure in question is incurred whether the appeal against the Pope's decrees, ordinances or laws is made to a future Universal Council or to a present Universal Council.

This censure is not incurred by appealing to a future Pope, nor is it incurred by appealing to a provincial Council by virtue of Canon 2332. It must be remembered that there is here a question of censures, and any law which establishes a censure must be interpreted strictly.[13] Sole [14] judiciously remarks, however, that an appeal to a provincial Council would be a much more atrocious insult to the Roman Pontiff, but this in itself is not sufficient to extend the application of a penal law beyond its proper bounds.

II.—Penalty for Disregarding Censures

It was also provided in the celebrated Constitution [15] of Pius IX that those who knowingly celebrate, or cause others to celebrate, divine offices in places interdicted by the Ordinary, by a delegated judge or by the law itself, or who admit those nominally excommunicated to divine offices, the reception of the Sacraments or to ecclesiastical burial, *ipso jure* incur an interdict *ab ingressu ecclesiae* until they have made proper satisfaction according to the will of him whose sentence they disregarded. This same provision of law is incorporated into the Code.[16] There are, however, some modifications. Hence, there is no longer any mention of the phrase "de locis ab Ordinario, vel delegato judice vel

[12] Sole, *loc. cit.*

[13] Can. 19.

[14] *Loc. cit.*

[15] Cons. "Apostolicae Sedis" Oct. 12, 1869, VI, n. 2 (*Fontes*, n. 552).

[16] Can. 2338, §3.

a jure interdictis;" but the Code simply uses the general phrase "in locis interdictis." [17] Another modification consists in the fact that Canon 2338, §3, makes no mention to the effect that an interdict *ab ingressu ecclesiae* is incurred by those who admit nominally excommunicated persons to the reception of the Sacraments. It is, however, provided in Canon 2338, §3, that they incur this censure who admit to the celebration of divine offices such clerics as have sustained a declaratory or condemnatory sentence of excommunication, suspension or interdict.

It is clear that the term *celebrantes* can mean only clerics, since only clerics can celebrate divine offices. Exception is made, however, in favor of Bishops by reason of Canon 2227, §2; consequently, they do not incur this penalty.

Of course the penalty under consideration is not incurred if ignorance can be pleaded, provided the ignorance is not affected.[18] It must be remembered, however, that affected ignorance never excuses from incurring the penalty. The penalty in question is not incurred when the celebration of divine offices or the permission to celebrate them take place in places under interdict, if the celebration of the divine offices takes place by virtue of the provisions of Canons 2270 ff.[19]

The term "admittentes" includes only those whose duty it is to permit or prohibit a cleric to the celebration of divine offices. Hence, pastors and rectors, and other clerics having charge of churches are included here.

It is to be noted that Canon 2338, §3, provides that the interdict *ab ingressu ecclesiae* is incurred by those who admit clerics under censure to the celebration of divine offices. Consequently, it is patent that that one does not incur this penalty by admitting a cleric who is bound by a vindictive penalty.[20] Nor is the penalty incurred if there has been no condemnatory or declaratory sentence issued against the censured cleric who has been admitted to the celebration of divine offices.

---

[17] Can. 2338, §3.

[18] Can. 2229, §1, §2.

[19] Vermeersch-Creusen, *Epitome*, III, n. 537.

[20] Augustine, *Commentary*, VIII, 355 ff.

III.—Penalty Against Those Causing Interdicts

The Code justly provides in Canon 2338, §4, that they who by their delicts have caused a local interdict or a general personal interdict to be imposed, *ipso facto* incur a personal interdict. Since this interdict is contracted by each guilty individual as such, it is clear that it is a particular personal interdict.

This regulation is by no means new, but was in force under the law of the Decretals.[21] Consequently, they become personally interdicted who were the instigators or the principals of the delict which caused the local or general personal interdict to be imposed. Hence, for example, those who caused a disturbance in a parish with the result that the Bishop imposed an interdict, automatically fall under a personal interdict. Consequently, they are subject to the privations attached to the personal interdict as set forth in Canon 2275. According to Cappello,[22] it makes no difference whether the local or general personal interdict becomes effective from the law itself, by a sentence from a competent judge or by a precept of a Superior. The reason for such a measure of discipline is because the legislator recognizes the fact that all who take part in committing a delict should be punished in proportion to their guilt.[23]

IV.—Penalty for the Extortion of Ecclesiastical Burial

The last clause of Canon 2339 has reference to an interdict *ab ingressu ecclesiae* incurred by those who knowingly and willingly grant ecclesiastical burial to those to whom it is forbidden by Canon 1240, §1; "...sponte vero sepulturam eisdem donantes, *interdictum ab ingressu ecclesiae* Ordinario reservatum." Thus, it is provided that they who, of their own accord, grant ecclesiastical burial to infidels, apostates from the faith, heretics, schismatics, *post sententiam* excommunicated or interdicted persons,[24] incur an in-

[21] C. 24, *de sent. excom.*, V, 11, in VI°.
[22] *De Censuris*, n. 403.
[23] Cfr. Canons 2209; 2219, §3; 2230; 2231.
[24] Can. 1240, §1.

terdict *ab ingressu ecclesiae* reserved to the Ordinary. This same provision was contained in the celebrated constitution of Pius IX.[25]

The Canon employs the term *sponte donantes,* which signifies that the granting of ecclesiastical burial must be done knowingly and freely, otherwise there is no penalty.[26] The term *donantes* includes only clerics, because only they can be said to have the authority to grant ecclesiastical burial. Hence, Sole writes: "Hoc interdictum solos clericos tenet, illos nempe ad quos spectat sepulturam donare; hinc alii clerici, qui more laicorum funus comitantur non tenentur hoc interdicto." [27] Those who incur this penalty are subject to the provisions of Canon 2277.

V.—Penalty Against Violators of Bodies or Graves of the Dead

According to Canon 2328, whosoever desecrates the bodies of the dead or their graves, in order to commit theft, or for some other evil end, is to be punished with a personal interdict, is *ipso jure infamis,* and if the offender be a cleric, he is to be deposed.

It is the earnest intention of the Church to insure reverence for the dead and their resting places. Consequently, one who violates the bodies or the graves of the dead, besides becoming *ipso jure infamis,* is to be punished with the personal interdict. This penalty, however, is not incurred *ipso facto,* and is, therefore, a *ferendae sententiae* penalty.[28]

As Augustine [29] judiciously remarks, it makes no difference whether the violated body be that of a criminal or of a respectable person; nor is it necessary that the grave be blessed. Moreover, the Code does not distinguish between the faithful and infidels, but uses the generic term: "Qui cadavera vel sepulcra mortuorum...violaverit," consequently, it would seem that the censure in question is in-

[25] Cons. "Apostolicae Sedis," Oct. 12, 1869, VI, n. 2, (*Fontes,* n. 552).
[26] Can. 2229, §2.
[27] *De Delictis et Poenis,* n. 485; Cappello, *De Censuris,* n. 485.
[28] Can. 2217, §2.
[29] *Commentary,* VIII, 318.

curred when the body or grave of any human being is desecrated. The motive must be theft, or any other evil design, such as hatred or revenge.

VI.—Penalty Against Violators of Churches and Cemeteries

It is provided in Canon 2329 that they who violate churches or cemeteries by any of the acts described in Canons 1172 and 1207 are to be punished by the Ordinary with an interdict *ab ingressu ecclesiae*, and with other penalties according to the gravity of the delict. Hence the interdict *ab ingressu ecclesiae* is to be inflicted by the Ordinary against those who violate a church. This violation takes place when any one of the acts enumerated in Canon 1172 is committed. It is necessary, however, that the acts be certain, notorious and committed in the church itself. Among these acts are: murder, causing injurious and serious bloodshed, making use of a church for impious and shameful purposes, and the burial in a church of an infidel or a *post sententiam* excommunicated person.[30] Although the penalty in question is *ferendae sententiae*, it seems that the Ordinary is not altogether free to inflict it or not; for Canon 2329 uses preceptive words.[31]

With regard to the desecration of cemeteries, consideration must be given to Canon 1207, which states that the provisions of the canons which legislate concerning the violation of churches, apply also to the violation of cemeteries. Consequently, the acts enumerated in the preceding paragraph about the violation of churches have application here. In this connection, Vermeersch-Creusen write: "Quia coemeterium locus est *sacer*, interdicto affici, violari et reconciliari potest."[32] Of course, the penalty for the violation of a cemetery is identical with that for the violation of a church, because Canon 2329 provides the same punishment in both instances.[33] Consequently, one who violates a cemetery by any of the acts enumerated in Canon 1172,

[30] Can. 1172, §1.
[31] Can. 2223, §3.
[32] *Epitome*, II, n. 517.
[33] Can. 1207.

§1, is to be punished by the Ordinary with an interdict *ab ingressu ecclesiae* and other penalties in proportion to the gravity of the crime. This penalty of interdict *ab ingressu ecclesiae* prescribed in Canon 2329 is *ferendae sententiae.*[34]

VII.—Penalty Against Bigamists

According to Canon 2356, bigamists are those who, although validly married, attempt another marriage, even if it be only the so-called civil marriage. Of course, it is understood that there is here a question of one who is in bad faith. Consequently, if a man's wife is still living, but he is persuaded that she is dead, and he attempts to marry again, certainly such a man is not a bigamist in the sense of Canon 2356. Accordingly, Vermeersch-Creusen write: "Bigamia est delictum ejus qui matrimonium attentat conscius vinculi matrimonialis quo ipse vel compars ligatur." [35] Augustine [36] adds that bigamy is punishable only when it is subjective; in other words, when one knows that the former marriage bond was, and still is, valid.

In this question of bigamy, care must be taken to distinguish between the laws of the State and the laws of God and of the Church; for the law forbidding bigamy arises from divine law. The State sometimes grants a divorce which in no wise dissolves the matrimonial bond. Thus, Vermeersch-Creusen write: "Ubi lex civilis divortium perfectum permittit, delictum bigamiae in lege poenali laica alio sensu atque in jure ecclesiastico intellegitur, nempe de eo qui, vinculo matrimonii civilis per mortem conjugis vel per divortium non soluto, novum matrimonium civile attentat." [37]

In order to be guilty of bigamy in the full canonical sense, there must be an attempt to contract a second marriage; in other words, there must be a semblance of mar-

---

[34] Can. 2217, §2.

[35] *Epitome,* III, n. 558.

[36] *Commentary,* VIII, 412.

[37] *Epitome, loc. cit.*

riage. Hence, the guilty party must go through a civil marriage ceremony at least, otherwise there is no censure.[38]

Those guilty of bigamy become *ipso facto infames.* If they fail to heed the monition of the Ordinary and continue to live in open immorality, they are to be punished either by excommunication or by the personal interdict.[39] It is clear from the wording of the canon just cited that the personal interdict prescribed for bigamists is *ferendae sententiae.* Moreover, this penalty is to be inflicted only after a warning from the Ordinary, and this warning should be given according to the provision of Canon 2309.

The Canon indicates from the phrase *pro diversa reatus gravitate* that the seriousness of the crime is to be considered in each individual case. Therefore, the crime of bigamy would be much more serious and would cause much greater scandal if committed by one of high rank or station.[40]

---

[38] Augustine, *Commentary,* VIII, 412.
[39] Can. 2356.
[40] Can. 2207, n. 1.

BIBLIOGRAPHY

SOURCES

Acta Apostolicae Sedis, Romae, 1909-
Acta Sanctae Sedis, 41 vols., Romae, 1865-1908.
Canones et Decreta Concilii Tridentini, Taurini, 1913.
Codex Juris Canonici Pii X Pontificis Maximi jussu digestus Benedicti XV auctoritate promulgatus, Romae, 1918.
Codicis Juris Canonici Fontes, 4 vols., Romae, 1923-1926.
Collectanea S. Congregationis de Propaganda Fide, 2 vols., Romae, 1907.
Corpus Juris Canonici, 2 ed., 2 vols., Lipsiae, 1922.
Corpus Juris Civilis, Berolini, 1922.
Denzinger-Bannwart, *Enchiridion Symbolorum*, Friburgi Br., 1922.
Mansi, *Sacrorum Conciliorum Nova et Amplissima Collectio*, 51 vols., Paris, 1901-1919.
Thesaurus Resolutionum Sacrae Congragationis Concilii, 167 vols., Romae, 1718-1908.

WORKS OF REFERENCE

Aertnys-Damen, *Theologia Moralis*, 10 ed., 2 vols. Buscoduci, 1920.
Alterii, *Disputationes De Censuris Ecclesiasticis*, Romae, 1616.
Augustine, Charles, *A Commentary on the New Code of Canon Law*, 8 vols., St. Louis, 1918-1923.
Ayrinhac, *Penal Legislation in the New Code of Canon Law*, New York, 1918.
Bellarmine, *Opera Omnia*, 5 vols., Paris, 1870.
Benedict XIV, *De Synodo Diocesana*, 2 vols., Romae, 1806.
Blat, *Commentarium Textus Codicis Juris Canonici*, 5 vols., Romae, 1921-1927.
Bonacina, *Operum Omnium de Morali Theologia Compendium Absolutissimum*, Lugduni, 1634.
Bouquet, *Recueil des historiens des Gaules et de la France*, Paris, 1869-1880.
Bouuaert-Simenon, *Manuale Juris Canonici*, 2 ed., Gandae et Leodii, 1926.
Caesar, *De Bello Gallico*.

Cappello, *Tractatus Canonico-Moralis de Censuris juxta Codicem Juris Canonici*, 2 ed., Taurinorum Augustae, 1925.

Cappello, *Tractatus Canonico-Moralis de Sacramentis*, 2 ed., 3 vols., Taurinorum Augustae, 1926-1928.

Catholic Encyclopedia, 15 vols., New York, 1917.

Cavagnis, *Institutiones Juris Publici Ecclesiastici*, 3 vols., Romae, 1882.

Cerato, *Censurae Vigentes Ipso Facto a Codice Juris Canonici Excerptae*, 2 ed., Patavii, 1921.

Chelodi, *Jus De Personis*, 2 ed., Trent, 1927.

Chelodi, *Jus Poenale*, Trent, 1920.

Cipollini, *De Censuris Latae Sententiae juxta Codicem Juris Canonici*, Taurini, 1925.

Cocchi, *Commentarium in Codicem Juris Canonici*, 7 vols., Taurini Augustae, 1925.

Coronata, *Jus Publicum Ecclesiasticum*, Taurini, 1924.

Crnica, *Modificationes in Tractatu de Censuris per Codicem Juris Canonici Introductae*, S. Mauritii Agaunensis, 1919.

D'Annibale, *Summula Theologiae Moralis*, 2 ed., Mediolani, 1881.

Demosthenes, *Orationes*, 4 ed. by F. Blass, Leipsig, 1901.

Devoti, *Libri IV Institutionum Canonicarum*, Leodii, 1860.

Dixon, *A General Introduction to the Sacred Scriptures*, 2 vols., Baltimore, 1853.

DuCange, *Glossarium Mediae et Infimae Latinitatis*, Paris, 1840.

Encyclopedia Brittanica, 12 ed., 32 vols., Cambridge, 1922.

Ferraris, *Prompta Bibliotheca Canonica*, 9 vols., Romae, 1885-1892.

Genicot-Salsmans, *Institutiones Theologiae Moralis*, 10 ed., 2 vols., Bruxellis, 1922.

Gury-Ballerini, *Compendium Theologiae Moralis*, 10 ed., 2 vols., Romae, 1889.

Haas, *Das Interdikt*, Bonn. 1929.

Hardouin, *Collectio Regia Maxima Conciliorum*, Paris, 1714.

Hefele, *Conciliengeschichte*, 2 ed., 9 vols., Freiburg Br., 1873-1890.

Hilarius a Sexten, *Tractatus De Censuris Ecclesiasticis*, Moguntiae, 1898.

Hilling, *Das Eherecht des Codex Juris Canonici*, Freiburg Br., 1927.

Hinschius, *System des Katholischen Kirchenrechts*, vol. IV, Berlin, 1888.

Holy Bible.

Howland, "*The Origin of the Local Interdict*," Report of the American Historical Association, vol. I (1899).

Hurter, *Storia d'Innocenzo III*, 3 vols., Milano, 1839.

Hyland, *Excommunication*, Washington, 1928.

Kilker, *Extreme Unction*, Washington, 1926.

Knecht, *Handbuch des Katholischen Eherechts*, Freiburg Br., 1928.

Kober, "*Das Interdikt*," in Archiv für Katholisches Kirchenrecht, XXI.

Krehbiel, *The Interdict*, Published by the American Historical Association, Washington, 1909.

Lea, *The Inquisition*, 3 vols., New York, 1887

Leage, *Roman Private Law*, London, 1924.

Lega, *De Delictis et Poenis*, 2 ed., Romae, 1910.

Lehmkuhl, *Theologia Moralis*, 5 ed., 2 vols., Freiburg Br., 1884.

Ligouri, S. Alphonsus, *Theologia Moralis*, 10 vols., Mechliniae, 1842-1845.

Lyszczarczyk, Venantius, O.F.M., *Compendium Privilegiorum Regularium*, Leopoli, 1906.

Maroto, *Institutiones Juris Canonici*, 2 vols., Matriti, 1919.

Migne, *Patrologia Graeca*, 161 vols., Paris, 1858-1864.

Migne, *Patrologia Latina*, 221 vols., Paris, 1847-1870.

Noldin, *Summa Theologiae Moralis*, 3 vols., Oeniponte, 1923.

Ojetti, *Synopsis Rerum Moralium et Juris Pontificii*, Romae, 1911.

Petrovits, *The New Church Law on Matrimony*, 2 ed., Philadelphia, 1926.

Piat, *Praelectiones Juris Regularis*, 2 vols., Tournai.

Quigley, *Condemned Societies*, Washington, 1927.

Reiffenstuel, *Jus Canonicum Universum*, 4 vols., Venice, 1735.

Richter, *Canones et Decreta Concilii Tridentini*, Lipsiae, 1853.

Schmalzgrueber, *Jus Ecclesiasticum Universum*, 12 vols., Romae, 1843-1845.

Smith, *Elements of Ecclesiastical Law*, 3 vols., 3 ed., 1888.

Sole, *De Delictis et Poenis*, Romae, 1920.

Solieri, *Institutiones Juris Ecclesiastici*, 2 ed., Romae, 1921.

Suarez, *Opera Omnia*, 26 vols., Paris, 1861.

Tanquerey, *Synopsis Theologiae Dogmaticae*, 19 ed., Romae, 1922.

Vacandard, *The Inquisition*, 2 ed. (Translated by B. L. Conway), New York, 1926.

Van Espen, *Jus Ecclesiasticum Universum*, Venetiis, 1769.

Vermeersch-Creusen, *Epitome Juris Canonici*, 2 ed., 3 vols., Mechliniae, 1924-1925.

Vlaming, *Praelectiones Juris Matrimonii ad Normam Codicis Juris Canonici* 3 ed., 2 vols., Bussum, 1921.

Wernz, *Jus Decretalium*, 3 ed., 8 vols., Prati, 1913.

Wernz-Vidal, *Jus Canonicum*, 3 vols., Romae, 1923-1927.

Woywod, *The New Canon Law*, New York, 1918.

Woywod, *A Practical Commentary on the New Code of Canon Law*, 2 vols., New York, 1926.

Zollmann, *American Civil Church Law* (Edited by the Faculty of Political Science of Columbia University), vol. LXXVII, New York, 1917.

PERIODICALS

American Ecclesiastical Review (*AER*), Philadelphia, 1889-
Apollinaris, Romae, 1928-
Archiv für Katholisches Kirchenrecht (*AkKR*), Mainz, 1857-
Jus Pontificium, Romae, 1921-
Theologische Revue, Münster in Westfalen, 1902-

ABBREVIATIONS

AAS—*Acta Apostolicae Sedis.*
Acta SS—*Acta Sanctae Sedis.*
Fontes—*Codicis Juris Canonici Fontes.*
MPG—Migne, *Patrologiae Cursus Completus, Series Graeca.*
MPL—Migne, *Patrologiae Cursus Completus, Series Latina.*

Universitas Catholica Americae

Washington, D. C.

FACULTAS JURIS CANONICI

1930

No. 56

DEUS LUX MEA

TITULI

QUOS

AD DOCTORATUS GRADUM

IN

JURE CANONICO

APUD UNIVERSITATEM CATHOLICAM AMERICAE

CONSEQUENDUM

PUBLICE PROPUGNABIT

EDUARDUS JACOBUS CONRAN

SACERDOS ARCHIDIOECESIS PHILADELPHIENSIS

JURIS CANONICI LICENTIATUS

HORA IX A. M. DIE XXIV MAII A. D. MCMXXX

TITULI

DE JURE CANONICO

I.	De Dissertatione.		
II.	De Historia Juris Canonici.		
III.	Canones	1-7	De Ambitu Codicis.
IV.	Canones	8-24	De Legibus Ecclesiasticis.
V.	Canones	25-30	De Consuetudine.
VI.	Canones	31-35	De Temporis Supputatione.
VII.	Canones	36-62	De Rescriptis.
VIII.	Canones	63-79	De Privilegiis.
IX.	Canones	80-86	De Dispensationibus.
X.	Canones	87-107	Generales Notiones de Personis.
XI.	Canones	108-117	De Clericorum Adscriptione Alicui Diocesi.
XII.	Canones	118-123	De Juribus et Privilegiis Clericorum.
XIII.	Canones	124-144	De Obligationibus Clericorum.
XIV.	Canones	145-195	De Officiis Ecclesiasticis.
XV.	Canones	196-210	De Potestate Ordinaria et Delegata.
XVI.	Canones	211-214	De Reductione Clericorum ad Statum Laicalem.
XVII.	Canones	487-498	De Notione Religionis, et de Erectione et Suppressione Religionis, Provinciae et Domus.
XVIII.	Canones	499-537	De Religione Regimine.
XIX.	Canones	538-586	De Admissione in Religionem.
XX.	Canones	587-591	De Ratione Studiorum in Religionibus Clericalibus.
XXI.	Canones	592-631	De Obligationibus et Privilegiis Religiosorum.
XXII.	Canones	632-672	De Transitu ad Aliam Religionem, de Egressu e Religione, et de Dimissione Religiosorum.
XXIII.	Canones	673-681	De Societatibus sive Virorum sive Mulierum in Communi Viventium sine Votis.
XXIV.	Canones	1012-1018	De Matrimonio in Genere.
XXV.	Canones	1019-1034	De Iis Quae Matrimonii Celebratione Praemitti Debent.
XXVI.	Canones	1035-1057	De Impedimentis in Genere.
XXVII.	Canones	1058-1066	De Impedimentis Impedientibus.

Tituli

XXVIII.	Canones 1067-1080	De Impedimentis Dirimentibus.
XXIX.	Canones 1081-1093	De Consensu Matrimoniali.
XXX.	Canones 1552-1568	De Notione Judicii et de Foro Competenti.
XXXI.	Canones 1569-1607	De Variis Tribunalium Gradibus et Speciebus.
XXXII.	Canones 1608-1645	De Disciplina in Tribunalibus Servanda.
XXXIII.	Canones 1646-1666	De Partibus in Causa.
XXXIV.	Canones 1667-1705	De Actionibus et Exceptionibus.
XXXV.	Canones 1706-1725	De Causae Introductione.
XXXVI.	Canones 1726-1746	De Litis Contestatione, de Litis Instantia et de Interrogationibus Partibus in Judicio Faciendis.
XXXVII.	Canones 1747-1836	De Probationibus.
XXXVIII.	Canones 1837-1857	De Causis Incidentibus.
XXXIX.	Canones 2195-2198	De Natura Delicti Ejusque Divisione.
XL.	Canones 2199-2211	De Imputabilitate Delicti, de Causis Illam Aggravantibus vel Minuentibus, et de Juridicis Delicti Effectibus.
XLI.	Canones 2212-2213	De Conatu Delicti.
XLII.	Canones 2214-2240	De Poenis in Genere.
XLIII.	Canones 2241-2285	De Poenis Medicinalibus seu de Censuris.
XLIV.	Canones 2286-2305	De Poenis Vindicativis.
XLV.	Canones 2306-2313	De Remediis Poenalibus et Poenitentiis.

DE JURE ROMANO

XLVI. The Periods of Roman Law.
XLVII. The Sources of Roman Law.
XLVIII. Slavery.
XLIX. Personality.
L. Citizenship.
LI. Patria Potestas.
LII. Personae in Manu.
LIII. Personae in Mancipio.
LIV. Tutela et Cura.
LV. Ownership.
LVI. De Obligationibus in Genere.
LVII. De Obligationibus Extra-Contractualibus.
LVIII. Furtum.
LIX. Damnum Injuria Datum.
LX. Injuria.

Tituli

Vidit Facultas:

PHILIPPUS BERNARDINI, S.T.D., J.U.D., Decanus.
LUDOVICUS H. MOTRY, S.T.D., J.C.D., a Secretis.
VALENTINUS T. SCHAAF, O.F.M., J.C.D.
FRANCISCUS J. LARDONE, S.T.D., J.U.D.

Vidit Rector Magnificus Universitatis:

JACOBUS HUGO RYAN, Ph.D., S.T.D.

VITA

Edward James Conran was born in Norristown, Penna., on February 17, 1903. Having attended the parochial school, he entered the Villanova Preparatory School, and later entered the Seminary of Saint Charles, Overbrook, Penna., receiving from the last named institution the degree of Bachelor of Arts. In September, 1928, he matriculated at the Catholic University of America, and commenced his graduate studies in the School of Canon Law, and received at the end of the year the degrees of Bachelor and Licentiate in Canon Law. He was ordained to the Holy Priesthood on May 25, 1929, by His Eminence Cardinal Dougherty. He wrote and published this dissertation in partial fulfillment of the requirements for the degree of Doctor of Canon Law, which was conferred upon him in June, 1930.

www.ingramcontent.com/pod-product-compliance
Lightning Source LLC
LaVergne TN
LVHW050226080826
844660LV00012B/479

9780813222455